# SHEPHERD'S NOTES

# SHEPHERD'S NOTES

## Bible Summary Series

# Manners &
Customs of
Bible Times

BROADMAN
&HOLMAN
PUBLISHERS

Nashville, Tennessee

Shepherd's Notes—Manners & Customs of Bible Times
© 2000
by Broadman & Holman Publishers
Nashville, Tennessee
All rights reserved
Printed in the United States of America

0–0854–9376–X
Dewey Decimal Classification: 220.9
Subject Heading: Jews—Social life and customs
Library of Congress Card Catalog Number: 99–054865

**Library of Congress Cataloging-in-Publication Data**
Enns, Paul P., 1937–
    Manners & customs of Bible times / Paul Enns.
        p. cm.    — (Shepherd's notes. )
    Includes bibliographical references.
    ISBN 0–8054–9376–X (alk. paper)
    1. Jews—Social life and customs—To 70 A.D.   2. Palestine—Social life and customs—To 70 A.D.   3. Bible—Antiquities.   I. Title: Manners & customs of Bible times. II. Title. II. Series.
    DS112.E56 2000
    220.9'5—dc21                                                                99–054865
                                                                                            CIP

123456   03 02 01 00
R

# CONTENTS

Dear Reader:

*Shepherd's Notes* are now available on every book in the Bible. In addition, we are pleased to provide a number of volumes in what we call **The Bible Summary Series**. This series will give you a perspective on various parts of the Bible that you wouldn't get by focusing on a book at time. These volumes include *Old Testament, New Testament, Life & Teachings of Jesus, Life & Letters of Paul, Basic Christian Beliefs,* and *Manners & Customs of Bible Times.*

This particular volume, *Manners & Customs of Bible Times* by Paul Enns, provides a quick and easy-to-read description of the cultures and practices that form the background in which events in the Bible took place. *Manners & Customs of Bible Times* complements other volumes of *Shepherd's Notes* including a number of volumes on Christian classics. You can find a complete listing of all *Shepherd's Notes* on the back cover.

It's our prayer that *Shepherd's Notes* will serve you well as you read and live God's Word.

In Him,

David R. Shepherd
Editor-in-Chief

## DESIGNED FOR THE BUSY USER

*Shepherd's Notes* is a complete library of resources designed for Bible study. Forty-one of the volumes provide an easy-to-use tool for getting a quick handle on a particular Bible book's important features and for gaining an understanding of the message of that book.

*Shepherd's Notes: The Bible Summary Series* complement and supplement *Shepherd's Notes* on individual books of the Bible. The present volume, *Manners & Customs of Bible Times,* enriches Bible study by closing the gap between the cultures and times in which events in the Bible took place with the twenty-first century.

*Shepherd's Notes* are for laypersons, pastors, teachers, small-group leaders and participants, as well as the classroom student. Enrich your personal study or quiet time. Shorten your class or small-group preparation time as you gain valuable insights in the truths of God's Word that you can pass along to your students or group members.

## DESIGNED FOR QUICK ACCESS

Those with time restraints will especially appreciate the timesaving features built in the *Shepherd's Notes*. All features are intended to aid a quick and concise encounter with the crux of the message.

*Concise Information. Manners & Customs of Bible Times* is arranged topically and is designed so that you can quickly get the information you need to understand better the portion of Scripture you are studying.

*Icons*. Various icons in the margin highlight recurring themes and aid in selective searching or tracing of those themes.

*Sidebars and Charts*. These specially selected features provide additional background information to your study or preparation. These include definitions as well as cultural, historical, and biblical insights.

In addition to the above features, for those readers who require or desire more information and resources, a list reference sources used for this volume suggests many works that allow the reader to extend the scope of his or her study.

## DESIGNED TO WORK FOR YOU

*Personal Study.* Using *Shepherd's Notes* with a passage of Scripture can help explain many passages that aren't readily understandable apart from the historical and cultural context.

*Teaching. Manners & Customs of Bible Times* will be useful in preparing to teach from almost any portion of Scripture.

## LIST OF MARGIN ICONS USED IN MANNERS & CUSTOMS OF BIBLE TIMES

 *Historical Context.* To indicate historical information—historical, biographical, cultural—and provide insight on the understanding or interpretation of a passage.

 *Old Testament Passage.* To indicate an Old Testament passage that illustrates the topic under discussion.

 *New Testament Passage.* To indicate a New Testament passage that illustrates the topic under discussion

 *Word Picture.* To indicate that the meaning of a specific word or phrase is illustrated so as to shed light on it.

 *Personal Application.* To provide a personal or universal application of truth relevant to a particular text.

# INTRODUCTION

Christians agree that the Bible is vital to our spiritual life. Through the teaching of Scripture we learn the message of salvation (Acts 16:31), and through the Scriptures we grow to maturity in Christ (1 Pet. 2:2). Since the Word of God is vital to our salvation and spiritual growth, it is equally vital that we understand the Word. But the Scriptures were written 2,000 to 3,400 years ago; moreover, the Bible was written in a culture very different from ours. How are we to understand these ancient writings from a foreign culture?

That is the purpose of this study. To enhance our understanding of the Bible, we must understand the culture in which the Bible was written. *Shepherd's Notes* for *Manners & Customs of Bible Times* is designed to remove the barrier of understanding by illuminating these aspects of ancient eastern culture:

- home life
- cuisine
- clothing
- educational system
- occupations
- city life
- religious system.

In plain words, a study of *Manners & Customs of Bible Times* will open your eyes in your future study of the Scriptures. You will understand anew the previously puzzling passages. Come and join us for an intriguing study of the customs of ancient Israel!

## HOMES

A home in Bible times was principally a place of shelter where people slept at night, but in the daytime the people spent their time working outdoors. Those who lived in tents were also nomadic; hence, their home was where they attended to basics—eating and sleeping—but their work was largely done outside, tending to their flocks. Wealthy people who owned larger homes used their homes more, which also included entertaining (Acts 1:13; 12:12; 20:8).

## CAVES

While not many people lived in caves in biblical times, some did. Caves were useful dwelling places: they were strong, ready-built homes; they afforded protection from wind and inclement weather. There were numerous caves throughout the land of Israel, including Bethlehem and Nazareth; in fact, it is likely that Jesus was born in a cave. After the Lord destroyed Sodom, Lot lived in a cave because he was afraid to live in Zoar (Gen. 19:30).

The caves at Qumran became hiding places for the Jews fleeing the Roman destruction of Jerusalem in A.D. 70.

Caves also afforded refuge. The kings who fled from Joshua hid in a cave (Josh. 10:18); in fleeing from Saul, David escaped to the cave at Adullam (1 Sam. 22:1). King Saul himself stayed in a cave while pursuing David (1 Sam. 24:1–7). At Mt. Carmel five hundred prophets hid in a cave because of Jezebel (1 Kings 18:4, 13). Elijah lived in a cave while fleeing from Jezebel (1 Kings 19:9, 13; cf. Heb. 11:38). In the tribulation people—including world leaders—will hide in caves, fearful of God's judgment (Rev. 6:15).

The Edomites had built an entire civilization in a community of caves at Petra. They were proud of their impenetrable location (Obad. 3). Even to this day some people live in caves. On the outskirts of Jerusalem laundry hangs outside of caves, a visible reminder of people living in the caves.

## TENTS

People living in tents dates back to the earliest beginnings of the Old Testament. Tents in biblical days were not square, nor did they have steep-pitched roofs; rather, they were rectangular, having several compartments and were a little higher in the center compartment. An average-sized, biblical tent was approximately ten feet by fifteen feet.

Originally made of animal skins, later tents were made of woven goat hair, black in color (cf. Song of Sol. 1:5). The goat hair cloth was woven in sections several feet wide, sewn together and held in place by poles. When the goat hair became wet, it shrank; hence, it was waterproof when it rained. On warm, sunny days the sides of the tent could be lifted for light and ventilation. The goat hair was thick, providing warmth and protection in winter weather.

Tents had at least two compartments, separated by a sheet hanging from the center pole. Women and children occupied one compartment while the men occupied the other compartment, which was also used for hospitality. In a three-compartment tent, the central compartment would be used for entertaining. Only the male head of the home was allowed beyond the hospitality compartment. It was unusual for Sisera, a visitor, to enter the tent of Jael (Judg.

We frequently evaluate people socially based on their house. How many square feet in your house? is a common question. How does our concept of determining the social standard of people based on the house they live in fit with Scripture? Consider that Jesus was born in a stable where animals were kept.

Read Genesis 18:1–15. Envision the scene. What can you learn about tent life from this event? What is in the tent? What activities occur in the tent? Where is Sarah? Where are Abraham and his visitors? How is Sarah able to hear them without being seen?

It is not uncommon for a married couple to be strapped with excessively high mortgage payments. How can believers maintain responsibility in providing a good home and yet be financially responsible?

Examine Mark 2:4. Explain the events surrounding this story from your knowledge of a biblical house.

"When they came down from the high place into the city, Samuel spoke with Saul on the roof" (1 Sam. 9:25, NASB).

4:18). Sometimes women and maids had their own tents (Gen. 31:33).

## COTTAGES

People in biblical times had a different concept of a house than modern people living in the Western world. Since most of the work was done outside, the house was merely a shelter and a place to sleep. Homes were built of clay bricks that had been dried in the sun. Snakes also enjoyed the warmth of the sun-baked bricks and would sometimes settle in the cracks—to the dismay of someone leaning against the wall (Amos 5:19)! Unlike Western, sloped roofs, Eastern roofs were flat. The roof itself was supported by beams and covered with thatched reeds and a clay coating (cf. Mark 2:3–5). The house faced into an open courtyard, with a fence (for protection) surrounding both the house and the courtyard. If a house had two rooms, the rooms were detached with a covered courtyard between them and an open courtyard extending beyond the two rooms. Animals would be kept within the courtyard, and a well or cistern providing water supply was also within the courtyard (2 Sam. 17:18–19).

An outside stairway alongside the house led to the roof which was used for many purposes. Grain and fruit were dried on the roof; it was also a suitable place for meditation and prayer, offering solitude and a cool breeze (cf. Acts 10:9).

Doors were made of sycamore, about six feet high. Doors were opened at sunup as a sign of hospitality and closed at sundown for security (cf. Rev. 3:8, 20).

An oil lamp was lit and placed on a stone shelf projecting from the wall to light the entire room

(Matt. 5:15). The lamp was lit and shone all night; only the poorest people would not light a lamp at night.

Like tent dwellers, people living in a one-room home bundled their bedding in the morning. In the evening the bedrolls were spread out on the floor with the family sleeping in a row, the father at one end, the mother at the other end, and the children in between. For this reason, to get up at night meant the entire household would be awakened (cf. Luke 11:5–7).

## LARGER HOMES

Larger houses were built in a U shape, opening into a courtyard where animals were kept. When a patriarch's son married, the father would add a room to an arm of the U, extending the home. The married son and his family would become part of his father's household. That is the imagery Jesus painted for believers in John 14:2.

Wealthy people would sometimes build an "upper room" on the roof, accessible by an outside stairway (cf. 2 Kings 4:10; Mark 14:15; cf. Acts 1:13). An upper room could be large—sufficient to host a big gathering (Acts 1:13–14; 12:12–17). People living in a large home would also have servants. Rhoda, a servant girl, responded to Peter's knock at the door, entering to the courtyard of John Mark's home (Acts 12:13).

"In my Father's house are many rooms; if it were not so, I would have told you. I am going there to prepare a place for you" (John 14:2).

Construct the scene in Acts 12:12–17. Indicate the location of the upper room. Locate the place where Peter is knocking.

"'It's no good, it's no good!' says the buyer; then off he goes and boasts about his purchase" (Prov. 20:14).

Examine Proverbs 11:1; 16:11; 20:10, 23. How should Christians conduct their business?

## THE MARKETPLACE

The marketplace was important in Eastern culture; it served not only as a place for transacting business but also as a social gathering place. Children played in the marketplace (Matt. 11:16); unemployed laborers sought work there (Matt. 20:3). Religious leaders congregated in the marketplace to receive people's accolades (Luke 11:43; 20:46). Because it was a place for social gatherings, Paul went to the marketplace in Athens and proclaimed the gospel (Acts 17:17). Sometimes official offices were near the marketplace, and legal matters were transacted there. In Philippi Paul and Silas were dragged before the authorities in the marketplace (Acts 16:19).

## BREAD

In biblical times people worked hard for the basic necessities of life. Bread and water were the two staple commodities. To bake bread, women ground the grain with a stone mill. Although the grinding could be done by one woman, usually two women sat facing each other (Matt. 24:41). Two stone cylinders, approximately eighteen inches in diameter were set on a cloth, one stone placed on top of the other, with a large hole surrounding the wooden pivot fastened to the bottom stone. A wooden handle was attached to the top stone which was rotated on the bottom stone. Grain was poured through the hole around the pivot, and as the top stone was turned, the grain was crushed and came out of the bottom as flour. Larger mills were turned by donkeys (cf. Mark

9:42); sometimes slaves were used to turn the larger mills, as Samson was used (Judg. 16:21).

Women were strong because of the hard work of grinding grain.

*Unleavened Bread.* Eaten in conjunction with their religious feasts, unleavened bread was flat, one-eighth to one-fourth-inch thick (Exod. 12:15; Matt. 26:23, 26; John 13:26).

*Leavened Bread.* The dough had leaven added to it. A pinch of leaven was always saved from one piece of dough for subsequent baking (cf. Matt. 13:33; Gal. 5:9). These loaves were larger, similar to the Western loaf of bread, but round. Bread made of barley was eaten by poor people, while wheat bread was a better quality (Judg. 7:13; Rev. 6:6).

*Smaller Cakes.* These small biscuits were eaten for lunch by an individual. These were the cakes Jesus used to feed the multitude (John 6:9).

*Baking.* Flour was mixed with water and salt; and in the case of leavened bread, the dough sat overnight until the leaven permeated the entire dough. In primitive baking the dough was simply placed on heated, flat stones (1 Kings 19:6).

Various kinds of ovens were also used. The flat bottom of an inverted pot placed over a fire was sometimes used for baking. Another was a circular metal sheet placed on stones about nine inches above the ground.

## WATER

Since much of the Bible land is desert, water was an important and precious commodity. Wells were dug with communities congregating around a water source (Gen. 24:10–11; 26:15, 18–22; 29:2–10). The wells supplied the people

"But a certain woman threw an upper millstone on Abimelech's head, crushing his skull" (Judg. 9:53, NASB).

Study Ezekiel's "acted parable" in Ezekiel 4:9–17. What can you learn from this incident? What were the economic conditions? Why had this happened to the Israelites? What application can you draw?

Eating together involves hospitality, trust, and fellowship. Considering this, what can you learn from Matthew 26:20–30?

Examine John 7:37–39. In the light of that culture, what significance did Jesus' words have? (See also Psalm 23:2).

What is the significance of the phrase "a land flowing with milk and honey" (Exod. 3:8, 17; 13:5; Josh. 5:6; Jer. 11:5)?

It was a special occasion when the angelic visitors came to Abraham (Gen. 18:7–8); it was a time of celebration when the repentant son returned home (Luke 15:23).

as well as the flocks of sheep and herds of camels with water.

Because of the heat, water was normally carried from the well in the evening when it was cooler. The well also became a place of congregating and visiting. Hence, the Samaritan woman came to the well at noon—during the heat—to avoid facing other women because of her reputation (John 4:6–7).

## MILK

Milk was a valuable food product and readily available from cows, goats, sheep, and camels (Gen. 32:15; Deut. 32:14; Prov. 27:27). Milk that thickened and soured became curds (yogurt), an important staple for the shepherd who took the warm milk out into the field in the morning; by the time he ate his lunch, it was curds (Isa. 7:15)! Jael gave Sisera a drink of buttermilk, which had naturally churned in an animal skin (Judg. 4:19; 5:25). This drink is still a staple in Bedouin homes.

Butter and cheese were also valuable byproducts of milk (Prov. 30:33; 2 Sam. 17:29). Butter was made by pouring milk into an animal skin and shaking it until it turned to butter.

## MEAT

Meat was rarely eaten; most people couldn't afford it; and, because of a lack of refrigeration, it could not be kept indefinitely. Once an animal had been slaughtered, the entire animal had to be eaten immediately. Further, a cow provided milk and was also used for plowing. Sheep provided both milk and wool. But when a cow or sheep was killed, the value of the animal in other provisions was also lost; hence, meat was only eaten on special occasions.

## FISH

Because of the Sea of Galilee and the Mediterranean Sea, fish were common and abundant. In preparation for eating, fish were boiled or roasted over coals (John 21:9–13). The people also learned how to salt the fish so they could be dried and kept for a period of time. The two fish that the young boy gave to Jesus were two tidbits, probably preserved fish (John 6:9).

Examine Genesis 18:1–15. How did Abraham treat his guests? What can you learn about hospitality? Can you draw any applications?

## FOWL

Ducks, geese, quail, partridges, and pigeons were eaten, normally roasted. Although chickens are not specifically mentioned as food, they were nonetheless in existence (Matt. 26:74–75). They were common food in neighboring countries; hence, it is likely they were eaten in Israel as well. Wild birds were captured by trapping them in a net (Amos 3:5).

## VEGETABLES

Vegetables were common; those most frequently eaten were beans and lentils (Ezek. 4:9). Lentils were a cereal made into a soup or stew (Gen. 25:34). Leeks (similar to onions), onions, and garlic were Egyptian staples (Num. 11:5). Cucumbers, melons, and gourds were also staples (Num. 11:5; Isa. 1:8; Jon. 4:6–10; 2 Kings 4:39). At Mahanaim, David's friends brought him, among other things, beans to eat (2 Sam. 17:28).

## FRUIT

Olives were one of the most valuable fruits. When crushed, they were used as oil in place of butter or fat (Lev. 2:5) for cooking (1 Kings 17:12). They were also eaten as a principal food. Additionally, olives served as both medicine and fuel.

Fresh grapes were also eaten as a fruit staple with bread. The land of Israel had an abundance of grapes (Num. 13:23). They produced wine, which—diluted four or five parts to one, became a normal beverage (Matt. 9:17; 21:33; John 2:1–11) and was particularly useful because of impure water (1 Tim. 5:23). Grapes were also dried, producing raisins (1 Sam. 25:18).

Figs were readily eaten and also baked into cakes (1 Sam. 25:18; 1 Chron. 12:40; cf. Matt. 21:19). A sour fruit, pomegranates were used in place of lemons (cf. Deut. 8:8; Song of Sol. 4:13; 6:11; 7:12). Wine was spiced with pomegranate juice (Song of Sol. 8:2).

## SPICES

Middle Eastern people favored spicy food. Black cummin and coriander substituted for pepper. Mint and anise were also popular spices. These spices were particularly used in stews.

## HONEY

Since there was no sugar, honey was the common sweetener. Bees built hives in rock crevices and trees: Moses found honey in a rock (Deut. 32:13; cf. Ps. 81:16); Samson scraped honey from a lion's carcass (Judg. 14:8–9); Jonathan found a honeycomb on the ground (1 Sam. 14:27); John the Baptist ate wild honey (Matt. 3:4). It is likely that Jews colonized bees in hives to produce honey.

## SALT

Salt was important for both flavoring food (Job 6:6) and for preserving food. Salt was also used in sacrificial offerings (Lev. 2:13) and in a meal, symbolizing an everlasting covenant (Num. 18:19). When salt lost its flavor, it was thrown

Study Jesus' unique words about salt in Matthew 5:13: "You are the salt of the earth. But if the salt loses its saltiness, how can it be made salty again? It is no longer good for anything, except to be thrown out and trampled by men."

How is the figure of salt used? What did Jesus mean? Why is "preservation" *not* the correct answer? Compare Colossians 4:6: "Let your conversation be always full of grace, seasoned with salt, so that you may know how to answer everyone."

out and mingled with dung to cause its decomposition (Matt. 5:13).

## MEALTIME

### Hand Washing

Since people ate with their hands, cleanliness was important. But ritual hand washing (Exod. 30:17–21) became obligatory for ordinary eating at mealtime. The Pharisees developed an elaborate ritual in what constituted hand washing to the extent that an entire tractate called "Hands" in the *Mishnah* is given to explaining proper hand washing. Proper hand washing, when hands were dirty, was in two sessions under running water. In the first effusion the arms extended upward whereby the water ran down toward the wrist (hands were only considered washed if the water extended at least to the wrists); in the second effusion the arms were held downward and the water ran off the fingertips. In wealthy homes the servant would pour the water for the guests (cf. John 13:4–5; 2 Kings 3:11).

The danger for true faith frequently centers on the outward and externals to the neglect of the internal. Note Jesus' discussion with the Pharisees over hand washing (Matt. 15:1–11). Compare and contrast the external versus the internal that Jesus emphasized.

### Eating

In an ordinary home the people would sit cross-legged on a mat (which served as a table), dipping into a common bowl (cf. 2 Kings 4:38–41). Common people did not own chairs and a table as is customary in the West, although sometimes a low table—just over a foot high—was used. The flat pieces of bread were used to dip into the common food bowl and make a sop. The bread pancakes were helpful in scooping up liquids (Ruth 2:14; Matt. 26:23).

Study Isaiah 25:6–12. What does this banquet picture teach about Messiah's kingdom? Note the material items mentioned: "banquet," "mountain," "aged wine," "nations," "tears," and others. What do these terms mean? Discuss these and explain them.

At banquets guests reclined around a table on a couch, resting on their left arm and using their right hand for eating (Luke 7:36–50).

Statistics indicate the average American family spends less than ten minutes together on an average day—including mealtime. Since mealtime is important for fellowship, what can the family do to nurture fellowship at mealtime?

Thankfulness is God's will for believers (1 Thess. 5:18). We sometimes think of God's will as something vague, but God's will is specific. Study Ephesians 5:20; Colossians 3:17; 1 Thessalonians 5:18. When and how will you apply these commands?

"Do not forget to entertain strangers, for by so doing some people have entertained angels without knowing it" (Heb. 13:2).

The banquet or feast was a symbol of dining in Messiah's kingdom (Matt. 8:11; Luke 14:15; 16:22). "Abraham's bosom" denotes reclining next to Abraham in the Messiah's kingdom (Luke 16:22, NASB).

### Prayer

Prayer, reflecting thanksgiving, was offered before meals (1 Sam. 9:13; Matt. 14:19; 15:36; 26:26; John 6:11). When Jesus "blessed" the food, it means He gave thanks for it (Matt. 14:19, NASB). The *Mishnah* prescribes the prayer of thanks concerning bread: "Blessed are you, O Lord, our God, King of the Universe, Who brings forth bread from the earth" (*Berakhot* 6:1).

## HOSPITALITY

### Obligation

Both Old and New Testaments vividly reflect hospitality as a sacred duty. Hotels and restaurants were not common in biblical days, hence travelers were dependent on others for hospitality. Offering a stranger a meal was more than providing food for him; it was a commitment to the stranger's safety and well-being. But a major reason for showing hospitality was the belief that visitors had been sent by God. Abraham reflected this sense of hospitality in providing a lavish meal for his heavenly visitors (Gen. 18:1–8). Lot went to wrongful lengths to protect his angelic visitors when he offered his daughters to the debased men at Sodom (Gen. 19:1–11). In a time of warfare, Jael betrayed her appearance of hospitality when she killed Sisera after offering him lodging (Judg. 4:17–21). The New Testament also admonishes believers to practice hospitality (Rom. 12:13).

## Greeting

There were several kinds of greetings in biblical times. One form was verbal, "Rejoice," "Hello," or "Greetings!" (Gk. *chaire* ) (Matt. 26:49; 28:9), or "Peace be with you" (cf. 1 Sam. 25:6, NASB; John 20:19). When Jesus sent them on their mission, the seventy bestowed the same greeting upon the household. This was more than a casual hello; it was a benediction, invoking God's blessing upon the household, particularly if they were God's own (Luke 10:5; cf. John 14:27).

There was also the customary kiss of greeting upon entering a home—grasping the person on the shoulders, drawing him near, and kissing him on the right cheek and then on the left (Luke 7:45). Samuel kissed Saul when he anointed him (1 Sam. 10:1). Paul admonished believers to "greet one another with a holy kiss" (Rom. 16:16). In Christian circles the kiss took on new meaning: it became a symbol of Christians' love for one another; it was "a kiss of love" (1 Pet. 5:14; cf. 1 Cor. 16:20; 2 Cor. 13:12; 1 Thess. 5:26).

Arab women and children kiss the beards of their husbands and fathers, who respond by kissing the forehead.

As a sign of affection, near relatives of both sexes would kiss one another (Gen. 29:11; Song of Sol. 8:1; cf. Gen. 27:27; 33:4; 45:15; Exod. 4:27; Luke 15:20).

When an honored guest appeared, people would bow in honor of the special visitor. Abraham bowed down in the presence of his divine guests (Gen. 18:2), as did Lot (Gen. 19:1). In purchasing the cave of Machpelah as a tomb for Sarah, Abraham bowed before the people (Gen.

Examine Genesis 19:1–2, "The two angels arrived at Sodom in the evening, and Lot was sitting in the gateway of the city. When he saw them, he got up to meet them and bowed down with his face to the ground. 'My Lords,' he said, 'please turn aside to your servant's house. You can wash your feet and spend the night and then go on your way early in the morning.'" What can you learn about greeting and hospitality from these verses?

How much thought do we give to the physical and spiritual well-being of people we meet? We frequently say, "How are you?" but we really don't want an answer! How can we develop a greater concern for the people we meet?

23:12). This practice is still common in Oriental culture today. When Cornelius prostrated himself before Peter, the apostle rejected the gesture, reminding him, "Stand up, . . . I am only a man being myself" (Acts 10:26).

### Washing the Feet

In biblical times it was customary to remove one's sandals upon entering a house. This was essential since the people would sit cross-legged on a rug, with the feet beneath the person; the sandals would soil both the clothes and the rug. Hence, when Moses approached the burning bush, the Lord instructed him to remove his sandals from his feet since otherwise he would defile the holy ground where he was standing (Exod. 3:5).

Upon entering a home it was customary for a servant to wash the visitor's feet, essential because of the dusty streets. The servant would pour water over the feet into a basin and wipe the feet with a towel. Jesus assumed the position of a servant when He washed the proud disciples' feet, giving them a vital lesson in life and service (John 13:1–15).

### Entertaining

In entertaining, the guest was received into the central compartment of the tent which was the reception area. For example, when Abraham hosted his divine visitors in the reception compartment, Sarah was listening in the women's compartment (Gen. 18:9–10). Men would dine with the male visitor and also sleep with him in this compartment; it was considered ill-mannered to allow the visitor to sleep alone. In a single-room cottage, the visitor would dine in the same room where everyone also slept. Sometimes a village had a public guest room where only male visitors were accommodated. If a family was traveling, they would wait at a public well or the city gate until someone invited them to stay in their home (Gen. 24:13–14; Judg. 19:15). In a larger house a separate room was provided for the guest (2 Kings 4:10).

## BANQUETS

### Invitation

There were two invitations to the banquet, one well in advance of the event and another the day of the banquet—each by a special messenger. Jesus illustrated the banquet invitation in the parable of the marriage feast (Matt. 22:1–13). The second invitation went to "those who had been invited," but they scorned the invitation (Matt. 22:3). This was a most serious breach of etiquette, and the host would not take this lightly (Matt. 22:7–13).

To accept the first invitation and scorn the second was the height of insult—tantamount to war.

### Arrangement at the Table

Banquets were reserved for special occasions of celebration—a wedding (Matt. 22:2), the visit of special guests (Gen. 18:1–8), the return of a son (Luke 15:22–24). During early Old Testament times, people ate formal meals while sitting cross-legged on a mat; later, during the kingdoms of Israel and Judah, people sat at a table on chairs or on couches. But in New Testament times the guests reclined on a triclinium—couches for three around a low U-shaped table. The guests would lie on their left side, with their head toward the table and their legs away from the table, supporting themselves on their left arm while using the right hand for eating. In that way a servant could wash the guests' feet (Luke 7:36–38). In this position the guests reclined facing the back of the person beside. Hence, John was reclining on Jesus' right side,

At the Last Supper Judas had the chief place of honor. In this way Jesus could have spoken to Judas, identifying him as the traitor without the other apostles hearing it (Matt. 26:25). Since Judas was in the place of honor, Jesus gave him a sop, a special indication of favor—here probably a last offer of grace (John 13:26).

As Jesus offered the sop as a final offer of grace to Judas, so there comes a final offer of grace—the last time an unbeliever hears the gospel before death. It could be that you have never trusted Jesus Christ as your personal Savior. This could be your last offer of grace. Why delay? Do not go out into the eternal night of darkness. Trust the Savior today!

This position in dining is both a picture of the believer's bliss in heaven (Luke 16:22) and the millennial kingdom (Matt. 8:11).

described as "reclining on Jesus' bosom" (John 13:23, NASB). A servant would serve food and wait on the guests. In homes the place of honor was on the raised platform, while others reclined at the lower level. The host reclined at the junction of the two U arms with places of honor at his right and his left. The chief place of honor was at the host's left.

### Dining

The banquet was lavish. Musicians were frequently present, playing their musical instruments (cf. Amos 6:5). Wine was served (Amos 6:6). The choicest lambs from the flock were roasted and eaten (1 Sam. 9:24), along with cheeses, vegetables, dates, honey, and figs. Dancing was also provided for entertainment (dancing was individual) (Mark 6:22). A cloth was hung from the house throughout the preliminary three courses of the meal, signaling that the invited guests were welcome. Sometimes poor people from the street were invited to the banquet (Matt. 22:9).

During the banquet the host would dip a piece of flat, pancake-type bread (torn from a large "sheet" of bread) into the common bowl of lamb, herbs, and spices and make a "sop" and give it to the guest (cf. John 13:26). The Passover *haroseth* was a sauce of raisins, dates, and sour wine, sometimes a side dish used by three or four people (Mark 14:20).

Guests ate with their fingers; spoons were used only for soup. There were no forks. There is a saying in the Middle East, "Why should a man use a fork when he has so many fingers?

# CLOTHING

## TUNIC

The tunic was an undergarment made of leather, goat hair, wool, linen, or cotton and worn next to the skin. It had no sleeves, and a man's tunic reached his knees while a woman's tunic reached her ankles.

## OUTER TUNIC OR ROBE

The robe was similar to the tunic except that it was longer and had sleeves. Some were fancy (Gen. 37:3). Some also had long, pointed sleeves that nearly reached to the ground.

## CLOAK

The cloak was an overcoat. It was a looser, longer garment, without sleeves. The cloak also served as a shepherd's and peasant's bedding and blanket at night. Therefore, if a cloak was given as insurance against a loan, it had to be returned by evening (Exod. 22:26–27). Paul likely requested his cloak because it was cold and damp in the Roman dungeon (2 Tim. 4:13).

## GIRDLE (SASH)

Sashes are still commonly sold in the marketplace in Jerusalem today. In biblical times the girdle or sash was made of leather, six inches wide, and tied around the waist (2 Kings 1:8; Matt. 3:4). More expensive ones were a handbreadth in width and made of cotton or even silk (Jer. 13:1). Travel was expedited by tying the robe around the body (the "loins," meaning the waist) with the girdle, making walking or running easier (Exod. 12:11; 1 Kings 18:46).

"Now Israel loved Joseph more than all his sons, because he was the son of his old age; and he made him a varicolored tunic" (Gen. 37:3, NASB).

How is Peter applying the physical binding of the sash around the waist to a spiritual principle in the phrase "gird up the loins of your mind" in 1 Peter 1:13, KJV? See also Ephesians 6:14.

## HEADDRESS OR TURBAN

Although the levitical priests wore turbans in their ministry (Exod. 28:4, 40; Ezek. 24:17), Israelites generally did not wear turbans or head coverings, apart from a cloth wrapped around the head.

## SANDALS

Sandals were made of leather (sometimes wood) and tied to the feet with thongs. They were removed before entering a home or a sacred site (Exod. 3:5; Josh. 5:15). Slaves removed the sandals and washed the feet of those in wealthy homes or people of respect (Matt. 3:11, NASB). Poor people and also those in mourning walked barefoot (2 Sam. 15:30). Prophets frequently reflected a message in walking barefoot (Isa. 20:2; Ezek. 24:17, 23).

"A woman must not wear men's clothing, and a man must not wear women's clothing. The LORD your God detests people who do this" (Deut. 22:5, NLT).

## MEN AND WOMEN DISTINCTIONS

The Mosaic Law commanded that women's clothing was to be distinct from men's clothing (Deut. 22:5); however, the distinction was more in detail rather than in kind. While women wore tunics and robes like men, women's clothing was more elaborate; their tunics were longer and their clothing fancier.

Hebrew women had greater freedom in Bible times than Arab women have today. The Egyptians saw Sarah's face (Gen. 12:14); Eli saw Hannah's mouth moving in prayer (1 Sam. 1:12). Older women were less likely to be veiled than younger women.

## VEIL

The veil was distinctive for women in biblical times and is, in fact, worn by Arab women to this day. (When this writer attempted to take a picture of an Arab woman in a Jerusalem market, she veiled her face.) When a man approached a woman in public, she would cover her face with the veil (Gen. 24:64–65). Women wore several kinds of veils. One, like a shawl or wrap, covered the face and also the upper part of the body. This was the type of shawl with which Rebekah veiled herself in Isaac's presence (Gen. 24:65). Tamar veiled herself with a shawl when Judah approached (Gen. 38:14, 19). Solomon's bride complained that the guardsmen took her shawl ("veil," KJV) away from her (Song of Sol. 5:7, NASB). When the woman's face was not veiled, the shawl could be thrown over her shoulder.

In normal housekeeping activities the women were unveiled, but in public they were normally veiled. Yet it is apparent that Hebrew women had more freedom than women in Arab communities today. Sarah was unveiled, enabling the Egyptians to recognize her beauty (Gen. 12:14); Abraham's servant saw Rebekah unveiled at the well (Gen. 24:15–16). Young women, especially those engaged to be married, were veiled in public; married women were not always veiled in public.

"You shall have no other gods before me" (Exod. 20:3).

"Honor your father and your mother, so that you may live long in the land the LORD your God is giving you" (Exod. 20:12).

Is there a relationship between the first commandment (Exod. 20:3) and the fifth commandment (Exod. 20:12)? How does a son's ridicule of an earthly father affect his attitude toward God the heavenly Father?

## FATHER

In contrast to modern families which constitute father, mother, and children, biblical families extended to grandchildren and servants as well as aunts, uncles, and cousins. They were extended families. In this patriarchal system the father was the head of the home. It was, in fact, a miniature kingdom with the father ruling the family clan. The authority and honor accorded the father is evident in the fifth commandment, "Honor your father and your mother" (Exod. 20:12). The father's authority was absolute; he could even initiate the death penalty against a rebellious son (Deut. 21:18–21).

## SUCCESSION

Normally, the eldest son assumed the headship of the family clan upon the death of the father. Isaac received the blessing and patriarchal inheritance from Abraham since he was the son of promise, born to Sarah (Gen. 21:1–7; 25:5, 11). Because Esau despised his birthright, Jacob received the blessing and the rights that normally fell to the eldest son (Gen. 25:23; 27:1–29).

## MOTHER AND WOMEN

### Position in Culture

Women were subordinate to men in biblical times. They prepared the meals; Abraham instructed Sarah to prepare the meal for their visitors (Gen. 18:6). In socializing, women were separated from the men. Sarah was not permitted to join the men in discussion; rather, she listened from the women's compartment in the tent (Gen. 18:9–10).

Women worked physically, grinding the grain (Matt. 24:41) and putting up the tents; hence, Jael was familiar with a hammer and tent peg, easily able to drive it through Sisera's head (Judg. 4:17–21)! Women also baked the bread (Lev. 26:26; Jer. 7:18), made the clothes and washed them. They carried water (Gen. 24:11; 1 Sam. 9:11; John 4:7), hence, it was unusual to see a man carrying a jar of water (Luke 22:10). Women watered the camels (Gen. 24:19); they worked in the fields, harvesting the grain (Ruth 2:2). In Arab culture today it is still common for women to do the field work. On driving through the West Bank in Israel visitors may see women working in the fields.

"Her children rise up and bless her; Her husband also, and he praises her, saying: 'Many daughters have done nobly, But you excel them all.' Charm is deceitful and beauty is vain, But a woman who fears the LORD, she shall be praised. Give her the product of her hands, And let her works praise her in the gates" (Prov. 31:28–31, NASB).

In public banquets the women ate separately from the men (Esther 1:9). They did not assume positions of public office. When Isaiah declares, "women rule over them" he is chiding the nation for inept male leadership (Isa. 3:12). On a journey men would ride while the women walked. In public women would walk behind the men. In their flight from Sodom, Lot's wife walked behind him (Gen. 19:26, NASB).

### Respect

Wives and mothers were respected in Israelite culture (Prov. 31:26). Isaac loved Rebekah (Gen. 24:67), and Jacob loved Rachel—so much so that he was willing to work for her for seven years (Gen. 29:18)! Paul instructed husbands to love and cherish their wives in the same way that Christ loved the church (Eph. 5:25, 29).

How can biblical counsel concerning marriage strengthen homes in our time?

## CHILDREN

### Blessing of God

Children were viewed as a blessing and gift from God (Ps. 113:9; 127:3) and pictured as arrows in a quiver. The man whose quiver was full of arrows was truly blessed (Ps. 127:4–5)! The wife of one who was blessed of God would have many children, pictured as olive plants around a table (Ps. 128:3). Hence, it was a calamity if a wife were childless (1 Sam. 1:5–8). But when the wife became pregnant, it was a sign that God had removed the reproach and was blessing the home (Luke 1:25).

### Significance of Male Children

Each home was a kingdom of its own with the father as the head in that patriarchal system. When the father died, the oldest son became heir and ruler of the family clan. The male descendants perpetuated the family clan, hence, there was a preference for male children. When a young man married, he brought his wife to his father's house, and the children born to them perpetuated the family lineage. Hence, when daughters were born to a household, they worked in the home during their early years; but when they married, they left the parental home for their husband's home. Additionally, every Hebrew mother rejoiced at the birth of a son, hoping the son would be the promised Messiah (Num. 24:17; Gen. 49:10).

How has the "two and no more" (children) affected our attitude and thinking about children? How has the mother's working at an outside job affected our view of children? Are children an asset or a liability? What does abortion say about our view of children?

### Birth of a Child

Midwives attended the birth of a child (Gen. 35:17; 38:28; Exod. 1:15–19). A birth stool was also used, with the mother crouching on the birth stool or on a pair of stones in giving birth (Exod. 1:16).

As soon as a child was born, the navel cord was cut, and the midwife rubbed the new child with salt (Ezek. 16:4). Salting the newborn not only helped firm the skin but was also an antiseptic. Then the baby was washed, rubbed with oil, and wrapped tightly in strips of cloth, four to five inches wide, for seven days. With the arms bound tightly at the side, the child was unable to move. Hebrews believed that the child's limbs would grow straight and strong by being wrapped tightly. After the clothes were removed, the child was again washed and rubbed with oil and wrapped with clothes for another seven days. This was repeated until the fortieth day. Mary similarly wrapped Jesus in "swaddling clothes" (Luke 2:7).

## Circumcision

On the eighth day after birth, Hebrew boys were circumcised (Lev. 12:3)—usually by the father (Gen. 17:23), but sometimes by a fellow Hebrew. Naming the child coincided with circumcision (Luke 1:59). Circumcision had great significance to the Hebrew people. It was a sign that they were in a special covenant relationship with the Lord (Gen. 17:10–11). Those that were not circumcised were cut off from the people because they had broken God's covenant (Gen. 17:14). Any male who became a Hebrew proselyte had to be circumcised to come under the umbrella of God's covenant with Israel.

Upon the birth of a male child, the mother was considered unclean for seven days, and after the circumcision of the boy on the eighth day, the mother remained at home for thirty-three days for her purification (Lev. 12:1–4). When a female child was born, the mother was unclean for fourteen days, followed by sixty-six days of purification (Lev. 12:5). The uncleanness related to the mother's bleeding. Following the time of purification, the mother went to the Temple to offer a lamb for a burnt offering and a young pigeon or a turtledove for a sin offering

(Lev. 12:6). Following this the mother was considered clean.

### Naming a Child

Names were important and had significant meaning since the name expressed the nature of the person. The mother frequently named the child (Gen. 29:32–30:24), but so did the father (Gen. 16:15; Exod. 2:22). Sometimes the circumstances of the birth factored into the name. When Rebekah gave birth to twins, the first son born was red and hairy, so he was named Esau, meaning "hairy" (Gen. 25:25). His descendants were the Edomites, meaning "red." The second son born to Rebekah grasped Esau's heel, so he was called Jacob, actually meaning "may He [God] protect," but the similarity of sound led to the meaning of "one who takes by the heel" or "supplants" (Gen. 25:26). As she was dying, Rachel named her son Ben-oni, meaning "son of my sorrow," but his father Jacob called him Benjamin, which can mean "son of my right hand" (Gen. 35:18). Nabal, whose name means "fool," fulfilled the meaning of his name when he foolishly opposed David (1 Sam. 25).

Isaiah's son Shear-Jashub, meaning "a remnant shall return" was a reminder to Judah that the impending Syrian-Israelite invasion would not destroy them (Isa. 7:3). Isaiah's son Maher-Shalal-Has-Baz, meaning "swift is the booty, speedy is the prey" was an encouragement to Judah that Assyria would quickly destroy Judah's nemesis, the Syrian-Israelite alliance (Isa. 8:3–4).

Frequently given names incorporated the name of God, particularly the name of Yahweh [Jehovah]. *Jehoahaz* means "Jehovah has laid hold of" (2 Kings 10:35). (They didn't always live up to their names.) *Joash* means "Jehovah has given" (2 Kings 11:2); *Jehohanan* means "Jehovah is favorable" (Ezra 10:28); *Jehoiachin* means "Jehovah will establish" (2 Kings 24:8). *Jeremiah*, the major prophet, means "Jehovah will lift up" (Jer. 1:1). *Ezekiel* means "God will strengthen," suggesting the courage God would give Ezekiel in ministering to his depraved culture (Ezek. 1:3).

Do we give any thought to naming our children? How do we name them? Why do we name them the names we do?

## SLAVES

In ancient Israel slavery was frequently the result of victory in warfare when people were captured and taken as slaves (Num. 31:26–28; Deut. 21:10). But there were other reasons slavery existed. A person could become a slave as a result of indebtedness to another (Exod. 21:2); this could involve entire families (2 Kings 4:1; Matt. 18:25). By working for his master, the slave would pay off his debt. In another scenario, when a thief was caught and could not make restitution (which sometimes required a fivefold repayment), he was sold as a slave (Exod. 22:3). If a slave received a wife from his master and they had children, when the slave was freed, the wife and children remained the property of the master (Exod. 21:4).

The Mosaic Law provided strict rules concerning slaves to protect them; particularly, they were protected from oppressive masters (Deut. 23:15–16). An Israelite who became enslaved to another Israelite was not to be oppressed but treated as a hired hand (Lev. 25:39–40). On the seventh year the slave was to be set free (Exod. 21:2; Deut. 15:12–18).

Slaves were sometimes so well treated that they enjoyed serving in the master's home. Slaves who became loyal to their masters could choose to remain with their master. When the appointed time of their release occurred and the slave chose to remain, the master would bring the slave to the doorway of the house and pierce his ear with an awl (Exod. 21:5–6). Then the slave belonged to the master permanently.

Sometimes slaves exercised considerable authority. Abraham entrusted the choice of a wife for his son Isaac to his slave (Gen. 24).

Biblical instruction in slave-master relationships has significant application for today. Read Ephesians 6:5–9 and Colossians 3:22–25. These passages speak to employee-employer relationships. What can we learn from these Scriptures?

In the Roman Empire slavery was prominent, with fully half of the estimated population of sixty million being slaves. While Israelites were benevolent to their slaves, slavery in the Roman Empire was quite different. Under Roman rule people became slaves because of Roman conquests, and the captive slaves were frequently treated harshly. Sometimes, however, educated people became slaves, resulting in their becoming teachers or tutors of their masters' children. While slaves had protection under the Mosaic Law, under Roman rule they had none. The master had the power of life and death over his slave. A slave that stole could be branded on his face, designating him as a thief. The master could have his slave crucified at will. Similarly, when caught, a runaway slave could be branded or put to death. The slave was at the mercy of his master.

# MARRIAGE

## POLYGAMY

There is a common misconception that the Old Testament allowed for polygamy. The Bible records what people did, but it did not sanction everything people did. The fact is, most people in biblical times were monogamous, not polygamous. Sometimes the wealthy and prominent took multiple wives for themselves, the classic example being Solomon who had seven hundred wives and three hundred concubines (1 Kings 11:3). Polygamy began with Lamech who took two wives for himself (Gen. 4:19) and continued even with men like Abraham who took Hagar as a handmaid when Sarah didn't bear any children (Gen. 16:1–16). Jacob, the father of Israel, had two wives and two handmaids (Gen. 29–30), and King David "took more concubines and wives" (2 Sam. 5:13).

But polygamy was wrong and forbidden by Scripture. Kings were warned not to multiply their wives (Deut. 17:17). The foundation of monogamy lies in God's original commandment binding husband and wife together in a "one flesh" arrangement that multiple marriages or mates destroy (Gen. 2:23–24).

Study Genesis 2:23–24 with the consideration, "one man and one woman for life." How does this passage of Scripture and this truth reflect a couple's commitment to their marriage?

## ARRANGED

In biblical times the father selected the bride for his sons. Abraham sent his servant to Haran to find a wife for his son Isaac (Gen. 24:1–4). He refused to allow his son to have a Canaanite wife; rather, he sought a bride for Isaac that was from Abraham's original home (Gen. 24:4). The bride became a part of her husband's family; hence, it was important that she would fit into her husband's culture. That was a primary reason the father selected the bride for his son. When Esau married a Hittite woman, the couple made life miserable for Isaac and Rebekah (Gen. 26:35).

Marriage occurred at a young age in biblical times. Eventually the rabbis established twelve as the minimum age for marriage for girls and thirteen for boys.

The Western world is concerned about love in marriage. In the ancient world love frequently came *after* marriage. Why were their marriages more stable than ours are today? What is love? How important is love in marriage? How do we mature in loving our spouse?

Despite the parents' arranging the marriage, love existed. Isaac loved Rebekah (Gen. 24:67); and even before they were married, Jacob loved Rachel (Gen. 29:18). Michal, Saul's daughter, loved David and "the thing was agreeable to him" (1 Sam. 18:20, NASB).

## PROHIBITIONS

Certain restrictions in marriage existed. Hebrews were prohibited from marrying near relatives. A man was prohibited from marrying his mother, sister, granddaughter (or daughter), aunt, daughter-in-law, sister-in-law, or step-daughter, among others (Lev. 18:6–18).

Examine 2 Corinthians 6:14–18 where God commands, "Do not be bound together with unbelievers" (v. 14, NASB). This would have many applications, but certainly it would apply to marriage. God forbids believers to marry unbelievers. Are we faithful in guiding our children in this important biblical truth?

Hebrews were also prohibited from marrying outside the Hebrew faith. Marriage with Canaanites and other foreigners was forbidden for the obvious reason that these pagans would lead their spouses away from devotion to the Lord (Deut. 7:3–4). Samson's parents were upset when he requested his parents to get him a Philistine wife (Judg. 14:2–3). However, if a Gentile converted to the Hebrew faith, marriage was permissible (Ruth 1:4, 16).

## NEGOTIATION

In arranging a marriage, the bridegroom's family paid a price (Heb. *mohar* ) for the bride (cf. Gen. 34:12; Exod. 22:16). This may have been for several reasons. Children were viewed as workers; and since the bride would leave her father's home to live with her husband's family, the bride's father was losing a worker. A further reason may have been to ensure the bride would be cared for should she be widowed. The bridal price was determined by the social standing of the families. Gifts given at the wedding were distinct from the *mohar*. In the parable of the lost coin, the coins (Gk. *drachmas* ) likely represented the woman's dowry—which was also her life's savings (Luke 15:8).

## BETROTHAL

When the marriage had been arranged, the couple entered the betrothal period, usually lasting a year, and much more binding than an engagement of today. During that year the man prepared the home for his bride. The betrothal was established in one of two ways: (1) a pledge in the presence of witnesses together with a sum of money, or (2) a written statement and a ceremony with a concluding benediction such as "Blessed are You, O Lord our God, King of the world, who has sanctified us by His commandments, and enjoined us about incest, and forbidden the betrothed, but allowed us those wedded by *Chuppah* and betrothal. Blessed are You, who sanctifies Israel by *Chuppah* and betrothal." Before Israel's Exile the betrothal was ratified by a verbal promise (Ezek. 16:8); after the Exile the bride and groom's parents signed a covenant binding the couple together. In New Testament times the parents of the bride and groom met, along with others as witnesses, while the groom gave the bride a gold ring or other valuable item. And to the bride he spoke this promise: "See by this ring you are set apart for me, according to the Law of Moses and of Israel."

A betrothed couple were considered "husband and wife" even though they were not formally married and did not live together. Joseph is called the husband of Mary even though they are only betrothed (Matt. 1:18–19). Dissolution of the betrothal could only occur through divorce (Matt. 1:19).

The serious nature of the betrothal is evident. If a man had sexual relations with a woman betrothed to another man, they were both subject to the death penalty (Deut. 22:23–24). Had she not been betrothed, the man would have paid fifty shekels to the woman's father as a dowry, and she would have become his wife (Deut. 22:28–29).

## WEDDING

The wedding was largely a social event during which a blessing was pronounced on the bride: "May you, our sister, become thousands of ten thousands, and may your descendants possess the gate of those who hate them" (Gen. 24:60, NASB). The blessing reflected the concept of God's blessing, namely, a large family and victory over one's enemies. The marriage itself was secured by the formalizing of a marriage contract.

The parable of the ten virgins is rich with explanation of the Jewish wedding (Matt. 25:1–13). The wedding ceremony began with the bridegroom bringing home the bride from her parents' house to his parental home. The bridegroom, accompanied by his friends and amid singing and music, led a procession through the streets of the town to the bride's home (cf. Jer. 16:9). Along the way friends who were ready and waiting with their lamps lit would join in the procession (Matt. 25:7–10). Veiled and dressed in beautifully embroidered clothes and adorned with jewels, the bride, accompanied by her attendants joined the bridegroom for the procession to his father's house (Ps. 45:13–15). Isaiah 61:10 describes the bridegroom decked out with a garland and the bride adorned with jewels. The bride's beauty would be forever remembered. The bride and groom were considered king and queen for the week. Sometimes the groom even wore a gold crown.

### Wedding Feast

Once at the home the bridal couple sat under a canopy (Song of Sol. 2:4) amid the festivities of games and dancing which lasted an entire week—sometimes longer). Guests praised the newly married couple; love for the couple graced the festival. Sumptuous meals and wine filled the home or banquet hall (John 2:1–11). Ample provision for an elaborate feast was essential; failure could bring a lawsuit (John 2:3). The bridal couple wore their wedding clothes throughout the week; guests also wore their finery—which was sometimes supplied by wealthy families (Matt. 22:12).

On the first night, when the marriage was to be consummated, the father escorted his daughter to the bridal chamber (Gen. 29:21–23; cf. Judg. 15:1). The bride's parents retained the blood-stained bedsheet to prove their daughter's virginity at marriage in case the husband attempted any recourse by charging that his bride was not a virgin (Deut. 22:13–21; cf. v. 15).

## DIVORCE

Since marriages fail because of the sinfulness of human beings, the Old Testament allowed for divorce and prescribed certain procedures both for the protection of the woman and also to prevent chaos in Jewish culture (Deut. 24:1–4). When a man divorced a woman, he gave her a certificate of divorce (v. 3), which gave her a measure of lawful protection whereby the husband could not make further claims on her. Specifically, if the woman remarried and her

The beauty of the new Jerusalem is described as "a bride adorned for her husband" (Rev. 21:2, NASB).

In some cases the bride did not remove the veil from her face until the following morning. When Jacob thought he was marrying Rachel, in the morning he discovered his wife was Leah (Gen. 29:25)! At other times the veil was removed during the feast and laid on the groom's shoulder, and the pronouncement made, "The government shall be on his shoulders" (cf. Isa. 9:6).

Marriage is important to God. Marriage should not be entered flippantly or carelessly. It is for a lifetime. What can we do to strengthen our marriages?

Jesus did not take sides with either Hillel or Shammai; instead, Jesus taught the permanence of marriage (Matt. 19:1–9). The exceptive clause "except for immorality" (Matt. 19:9) refers to divorce during the betrothal period under Jewish culture—even as Joseph determined to do while he was betrothed to Mary (Matt. 1:19). Note the exceptive clause does not occur elsewhere (Mark 10:11–12; Luke 16:18; Rom. 7:2–3; 1 Cor. 7:39).

A serious question every married person should consider is: Am I committed to the permanence of my marriage? A further question might be: What is the spiritual foundation for the permanence of marriage?

second husband divorced her or died, the first husband was prohibited from again taking her as his wife (v. 4). The intent was to prevent divorce from becoming too easy; otherwise, divorce could become a legal way of committing adultery. A man might divorce his wife and marry another, only to conclude that he really favored his first wife. This law would prevent him from returning to his first wife.

A further question relates to the reason for divorce. A man could divorce his wife if "she finds no favor in his eyes because he has found some indecency in her" (v. 1, NASB). What was the indecency? By New Testament times there were strongly divergent views concerning the indecency that permitted divorce. In fact, the Pharisees sought to make it a point of contention with Jesus, inciting Him to take sides between the school of Hillel and the school of Shammai. The school of Shammai took a strict position, stating that the indecency was adultery, the only permissible reason for divorce. The school of Hillel took a liberal view, suggesting that a man could divorce his wife for virtually any cause: if she was found in public with her head uncovered, if she spoke to other men, if she burned the bread she was baking, if she was quarrelsome, if she failed to bear a child within ten years, if she was disrespectful of his parents, or if he found a more attractive woman!

## SICKNESS

In the Old Testament God promised health to the Israelites if they kept His commandments (Exod. 15:26). Many of the commandments in the Mosaic Law were designed to give the Israelites health—the commandment to rest one day of the week (Exod. 20:8–11); the commandments concerning moral cleanliness (Lev. 18) as well as the dietary laws (Lev. 11), separation from diseases like leprosy (Lev. 13–14) and many others. Sin is ultimately the cause of sickness and death because of the fall of the human race (Gen. 3:19). At times God judged the people with sickness because of their sin (Deut. 28:60–61). Undoubtedly, for this reason the disciples thought the man who was blind from birth was blind because of sin (John 9:1–2). Jesus refuted their false notion.

## MEDICINE

### Medicine in the Old Testament

Medicine was largely unknown in the Old Testament, and people did not normally consult physicians. It was believed that obedience to God's commandments would result in health; sickness was a sign of rebellion against God's laws. Hence, when Asa sought the help of physicians when he suffered from diseased feet, it was considered rebellion against God (2 Chron. 16:12).

Eventually beliefs concerning sickness changed. The thesis of the Book of Job is that sickness is not because of sin (even though Job's three "friends" thought it was; cf. Job 42:7–8). Isaiah the prophet (not the physicians) instructed

The Egyptians were advanced in the practice of medicine for their day, even dividing medicine into various specialties. They performed "brain surgery," drilling a hole into the patient's head to let the evil spirits escape; in the process healing sometimes occurred because the pressure had been relieved. Egyptians also practiced dentistry. But there is no indication that Israel adopted Egypt's medical practices—probably due to their stringent separation from the Egyptians during their sojourn in Egypt.

Various plants with healing qualities were used in medical practice. For example, garlic, mandrake, and rue were used to heal dysentery. Olive oil was used as a salve or ointment (Mark 6:13; Luke 10:34). Frankincense and myrrh were also employed in treating diseases. Wine mixed with myrrh had a narcotic effect, designed to ease the pain (Mark 15:23). Wine was also used for stomach ailments (1 Tim. 5:23).

Healing the sick was a sign pointing to the Messiah (Isa. 35:5–6). Study Matthew 8:14–17; 9:1–8, 18–35; 15:21–31; 20:29–34; John 5:1–9; 9:1–12; 11:38–44. What can you learn about Jesus' attitude toward the sick? What comfort can those who are sick draw from these passages?

Hezekiah to apply a poultice of figs to heal the boil (2 Kings 20:7). In referring to Israel's sin, Isaiah compared it to a sick body that needed healing (Isa. 1:6). Isaiah reflected a knowledge of basic medicine in mentioning healing wounds with oil and closing ("pressed") and cleansing the wounds, followed by bandaging. Midwifery was also common in the Old Testament (Gen. 35:16–19; Exod. 1:15–21). The use of quarantine was effective is limiting the spread of sickness to a mother and newborn child (Lev. 12:1–4). The root of the mandrake was thought to aid conception (Gen. 30:9–24).

### Medicine in the New Testament

Many debilitating diseases are mentioned in the New Testament. Among the most common were blindness, deaf and mute, leprosy, palsy, paralysis, lameness, and many others. (More examples are recorded of Jesus healing the blind than any other sickness.) Through contact with other nations, Israel practiced medicine in New Testament times; physicians were common and numerous (Matt. 9:12; Mark 5:26; Luke 4:23; 5:31; 8:43). Luke, a travelling companion of Paul, was a physician (Col. 4:14). While the physicians practiced medicine according to the Greek and Roman methods, medical ineffectiveness is apparent as the pages of the New Testament are replete with sick people. Interestingly, concerning the woman with the hemorrhage, Mark stated that she "had endured much at the hands of many physicians, and had spent all that she had and was not helped at all, but rather had grown worse" (Mark 5:26, NASB)—not commendable for physicians! But on the same incident Luke merely commented she "could not be healed by anyone" (Luke 8:43, NASB). Luke was not about to disparage his profession!

## DEATH

While the concept of life after death is not as clear in the Old Testament as in the New, it is wrong to say that Old Testament people did not believe in life after death or that the Old Testament does not teach eternal life. The recurring phrase "he was gathered to his people" (Gen. 25:8) suggests both life after death and reunion with loved ones (cf. Gen. 35:29; 49:29, 33). However, the Old Testament does not provide the detailed picture of life after death and heaven as does the New Testament.

The harsh reality of death was symbolized by loud wailing and lamentation. When all the first-born of Egypt died, "there was a great cry in Egypt" (Exod. 12:30, NASB). Wailing notified others that a death had occurred and reflected their great grief at the death of a loved one. Micah described the lament like that of a jackal and the mourning like that of an ostrich (Mic. 1:8).

The sorrow and grief over the loss of a loved one was dramatic and expressive. Walking and weeping, King David lamented, "O my son Absalom, my son, my son Absalom! Would I had died instead of you, O Absalom, my son, my son!" (2 Sam. 18:33, NASB). David's grief is evident in the repetition of "Absalom, my son." In this ancient culture professional mourners were hired to lament the deceased and to extol his greatness. Jeremiah called for the "mourning women" and "wailing women" to incite people to mourn (Jer. 9:17–18, NASB). These women would follow the funeral bier, shrieking their lament.

There were other symbols of mourning. Tearing one's clothes and putting on sackcloth were also

Many times sickness has no direct relationship to sin, but can we prevent some sicknesses by more stringent adherence to biblical truth? Since the believer's body is the temple of the Holy Spirit, what ramifications does that have? Medically, we know that smoking causes lung cancer and consumption of alcohol causes numerous illnesses like cirrhosis of the liver. But what about overeating and lack of exercise?

signs of mourning (Gen. 37:34–35). The death of Ezekiel's wife served as an illustration of the death of the nation; but because it portrayed the nation's sin, Ezekiel was instructed not to mourn his wife's death nor to follow the normal mourning procedures (Ezek. 24:16–17). From this it is evident that in mourning a Hebrew would uncover his head or even shave his head and throw dust on it (Josh. 7:6; 1 Sam. 4:12); he would go barefoot (2 Sam. 15:30; Isa. 20:2) and cover the lower part of his face (Lev. 13:45; 2 Sam. 15:30; Jer. 14:3). Hebrews would also show their sympathy to the sorrowing by bringing food to the surviving (Ezek. 24:17; Jer. 16:7; Hos. 9:4). Mourners also beat their breasts to express their grief (Luke 23:48).

Because of the vague understanding concerning the afterlife in the Old Testament, continuance of the family name was important. Life continued in the family clan. God promised Abraham many descendants who would live on in the land God had given the patriarch (Gen. 13:16; 15:18).

Even the Old Testament, however, teaches continuance after death. Daniel promised, "Many of those who sleep in the dust of the ground will awake, these to everlasting life, but the others to disgrace and everlasting contempt" (Dan. 12:2, NASB).

What is the significance of the New Testament statement, "We do not want you to be uninformed, brethren, about those who are asleep [dead], so that you will not grieve, as do the rest who have no hope" (1 Thess. 4:13, NASB). How does this impact a believer's grief? How do believers grieve?

Mourning involved not only wailing but also music—which sometimes led to disorder (Matt. 9:23). In New Testament times it was prescribed that even the poorest families should provide at least one wailing woman and two flute players. It resulted in a showy, noisy event, filled with commotion (cf. Matt. 9:23; Mark 5:38).

## BURIAL

Failure to bury a corpse properly by leaving it lying above ground was a great insult and misfortune, suggesting the deceased would not find rest (cf. Jer. 16:6).

Because of the hot climate of the Middle East, which caused the bodies to decompose quickly, burial normally took place within twenty-four hours of the death (Deut. 21:23).

The Hebrews cared for the body in death. Retaining the body in death was symbolic of the hope of resurrection. Hence, Joseph instructed his brothers to carry his bones from Egypt back to the land of Israel (Gen. 50:25). After he died, they cared for Joseph's body by embalming it and placing it in a coffin (Gen. 50:26). When King Saul was slain and his body abused, the people of Jabesh Gilead came and reverently took his body and buried it (1 Sam. 31:13). It was considered adding insult to injury to defile the body in death. Similarly, when Jesus' disciples heard that John the Baptist had been beheaded, they took the body and buried it (Matt. 14:12). The ultimate example of concern for a body in death is seen in the believers' care for Jesus' body. Joseph carefully took and wrapped the body in clean clothes and laid it in a tomb (Matt. 27:59–60); Nicodemus came to embalm the body (John 19:39–40) as did the women (Mark 16:1).

Several steps were taken in preparing the body for burial. The body was washed (Acts 9:37), anointed with spices and aromatic oils and wrapped loosely in a linen cloth (Mark 16:1; Luke 24:1; John 19:39). Then the body was wrapped in circular fashion with strips of bandages, the arms and legs wrapped separately

Hebrew people did not cremate their dead. Cremation—burning the body—was viewed as a symbol of judgment. God judged the king of Moab for burning the bones of the king of Edom (Amos 2:1); Achan's body was burned as a symbol of God's judgment (Josh. 7:25).

In New Testament times the dead were buried in any color of clothing. One rabbi was buried in red. He rejected white since it could appear he was happy but also black since it could suggest grief. Another was buried in white to show he was not ashamed of his works; yet another was buried with his stockings, shoes, and a walking stick to demonstrate he was ready for the resurrection!

Carefully examine John 20:1–10. Note the wording. John came first to the tomb and saw [Gk. *blepei*] the linen wrappings; John scanned the scene, but in semidarkness he didn't see much. Peter entered the tomb and saw [Gk. *theorei*]; he theorized what had taken place (v. 6). Then John also entered the tomb and saw [Gk. *eidon*]; the "light went on" for John (v. 8). He now understood what had happened. Jesus' grave clothes retained the shape of His body; although slightly collapsed, the narrow, bandage-type linen wrappings still intact. There was only one answer—Jesus had risen from the dead!

(John 11:44; 19:40). Spices, which were dry, were sprinkled between the linen cloths. The wrapped body was then carried to its burial place on a wooden stretcher, with family and friends following (Luke 7:12; Amos 6:10).

Poorer people buried their dead (Gen. 35:8; 2 Kings 23:6). Villages had graveyards outside the town limits; for this reason Jesus met the villagers of Nain leaving the town (Luke 7:11–12). Wealthier Jews did not bury their dead but placed them in rock chambers or in family sepulchres or caves (Judg. 8:32). Some of these rock chambers can be seen today in Israel. The garden tomb where Jesus may have been buried can be visited today. Upon entering the cave, visitors first see a small mourners' room. Attached to the mourners' room is a burial room with two ledges of stone opposite each other. The bodies were placed on these stone ledges. In Bethany, visitors to Israel may also see the traditional burial chamber of Lazarus.

When the bodies had decomposed, the bones were removed and placed in stone jars or coffers called ossuaries. These ossuaries could house the bones of several people.

# EDUCATION

## EGYPTIAN

Since Jacob and his family entered Egypt as a family clan but emerged 430 years later as a nation of more than two million, it is interesting to discover the educational standards of the Egyptians. Acts 7:22 says, "Moses was educated in all the learning of the Egyptians" (NASB). Unquestionably, Moses had the finest education available in that day since he was reared in the royal household (Exod. 2:10). Formal Egyptian education began in the third millennium B.C. with vocational training leading to the student's becoming a priest, a soldier, an engineer, or another vocation.

Since Egyptian life revolved around their religion, Egyptian education began in the temple. Their education emphasized learning skillful writing and hieroglyphics; and to accomplish this, students laboriously copied formal documents and studied writing for their lessons. The Egyptians used wise sayings which the students also copied.

Additionally, the Egyptians studied music and dancing (in the temple), geometry, astronomy, chemistry, arithmetic, architecture, and other disciplines. Egyptians also studied foreign languages such as Canaanite—which Moses may have learned in Egypt. As a prince, Moses was also personally tutored by a court official. In that capacity he would also have learned archery and horseback riding.

Unfortunately, it is difficult to determine what impact Egyptian education had on the Israelites—perhaps not too much since the

What is the significance of public versus private Christian education for our children? What are the advantages and disadvantages of public education? How does secular education affect the thinking of Christians?

Instruction would have been largely oral, handing down the traditions and truth of the Law. Scrolls were kept in the synagogues; privately held scrolls would not have been common. Nonetheless, writing existed very early, and some boys learned to write.

Israelites separated themselves from the Egyptians.

## HEBREW

In their early years children were taught by their mother. King Lemuel was taught by his mother (Prov. 31:1); Timothy was taught the Old Testament Scriptures by both his mother and his grandmother (2 Tim. 1:5; 3:15). Beginning as early as five and perhaps even three years of age, boys were instructed by their fathers until the age of twelve. Mothers taught their daughters domestic duties which including preparing food according to the dietary laws. The mother prepared the daughter to be a good wife and mother. Fathers, in addition to providing religious instruction in the home, taught their sons a trade (frequently agriculture). In wealthy families tutors were hired to instruct the children (2 Kings 10:1).

At age twelve, the son had completed his instruction in the Law. He became a "son of the covenant." In a ritual the father fastened the phylacteries on the arm and forehead of his son, indicating the son's devotion to the Law in mind and heart (Deut. 6:8).

In Hebrew homes this instruction centered around the Mosaic Law. The primary purpose of education in a Hebrew home was to know the Lord and His Law and to fear and reverence His great name (Deut. 6:7; Prov. 1:7). Hebrew education was not interested in culture and academics but training in holiness (Lev. 19:2).

The format of teaching was a question-and-answer method (Josh. 4:21–22). This method was designed to promote inquisitive minds concerning God's mighty acts, with the father detailing God's great deliverance from

Egypt (Deut. 6:20–25). When children saw the Feast of Passover observed, they questioned the meaning of the ritual. This prompted an explanation of God's mighty power in rescuing the Hebrews from bondage in Egypt (Exod. 12:26; cf. 10:2; 13:14–15). When God brought the Israelites safely through the flooded Jordan and placed the memorial stones in commemoration of the miraculous event, the children questioned the meaning of the memorial stones, prompting an explanation (Josh. 4:6–7).

The Lord instructed the Israelites how they were to teach their children. They were to teach about God's mighty acts of deliverance to their children and grandchildren (Deut. 4:9–10); they were to teach the Law with its commandments to the children. Moreover, it was to be a continuous, consistent teaching, in the morning and in the evening, formally and informally (Deut. 6:7; 11:19). The object of the instruction was to recognize the mighty acts of God, creating a reverence and fear of God that would result in a child's desire to obey God's law implicitly (Deut. 32:46; Prov. 1:7).

A vital question every parent must answer is, Am I faithful in teaching my children the truth of God's Word? Am I consistent and faithful in teaching my children, or is it a hit-and-miss method? How can I be faithful in providing a solid biblical foundation for my children so that they will never depart from God's truth (Prov. 22:6)?

## THE SYNAGOGUE

### As a Place of Instruction

While there is some debate concerning the time the synagogue was founded, it was likely during the Babylonian Exile (605–536 B.C.). Following the destruction of the Temple in 586 B.C., a need arose concerning Israel's worship system. The synagogue became the answer. Prayer became the substitute for the sacrificial offerings which were no longer possible.

The synagogue then principally became a place of instruction in the Scriptures and prayer. Alfred Edersheim indicates that Hebrew children began instruction in a school in their fifth or sixth year in schoolhouses or in synagogues. The children and teacher either stood; or, as became common adult teaching later, the children sat on the ground in a semicircle, facing the teacher.

Although most instruction was done in the home, when schools and synagogues developed, children attended formal classes. From the age of five until ten, the Bible was exclusively the children's textbook; from ages ten to fifteen, they studied the Mishnah, the traditions that developed concerning the interpretation of the Law. After the age of fifteen, the students studied in higher academies of the rabbis.

**Mishnah**

*Mishnah* is a Hebrew term that means "to repeat" and eventually (around A.D. 100) came to mean "to learn." In rabbinic Judaism *mishnah* referred to the teaching or learning about the oral law passed on by a particular teacher. Today the *Mishnah* usually refers to the collected edition of rabbinic discussions of the oral law.

Children began their study with the Book of Leviticus, followed by a study of the rest of the Pentateuch. From there the children studied the Prophets and finally the Hagiographa—the writings which also included the Psalms and Proverbs. School hours were purposefully fixed so the student would not be overworked; in summer the hours were shortened.

Sections of the Old Testament were copied, specifically for children. These included the history of Creation to the Flood and Leviticus 1–9 and Numbers 1–10:35. Jesus' childhood was set in this environment.

### As a Place of Worship

Jews built synagogues in towns throughout the land of Israel and throughout the Mediterranean region as places of worship. Since the synagogue was to be the prominent building in town, it was usually built on the highest point in town or at a main intersection, frequently with the front doors facing Jerusalem.

In the synagogue was a chest which was called the "ark" (not the ark of the covenant—that was undoubtedly destroyed by the Babylonians in 586 B.C.) in which the Scripture scrolls were kept. Nearby was a raised platform on which the reader and the prayer leader stood. One or two rows of stone benches ran along two or three of the synagogue walls. Once these were occupied, the remaining people sat on wooden chairs or on mats in the center of the synagogue. The "best seats," where the scribes and Pharisees sat, were prominently located in front of the platform facing the congregation (Matt. 23:6; Mark 12:39; Luke 11:43; 20:46). A lone seat, "Moses' seat," was occupied by a distinguished scholar (Matt. 23:2).

A local synagogue was supervised by elders with a body of at least ten men required to form a congregation. A layman served as "ruler of the synagogue" (Luke 8:41; Acts 18:8, 17). The ruler had oversight of the synagogue in general, maintained order during the service, and appointed the readers. An attendant brought the scrolls to the reader and later replaced them (cf. Luke 4:17, 20). He would also blow the trumpet three times at sunset on Friday evening, announcing the beginning of the Sabbath; and he was also responsible for flogging criminals who had been condemned (Matt. 10:17; 23:34; Acts 5:40).

A synagogue service followed this pattern:

1. An invitation to prayer in which the leader exclaimed, "Bless the Lord who is to be blessed." The congregation responded, "Blessed be the Lord who is to be blessed for ever." The recitation of

**Shema**

*Shema* is the Hebrew imperative which means "hear." It became the name of the confession of faith (Deut. 6:4–9) that begins, "Hear, O Israel: The LORD our God, the LORD is one" (Deut. 6:4).

the *Shema* followed (Deut. 6:4–9; 11:13–21; Num. 15:37–41).

2. The prayers followed. One individual who had been chosen, prayed. The congregation responded with the word *Amen*.

3. A reading from the Mosaic Law followed. Genesis, Exodus, Leviticus, Numbers, and Deuteronomy were divided into 154 parts so the Pentateuch was read in three and one-half years. At least seven readers took part in each service, each reading no fewer than three verses. Following the reading of a verse, an interpreter would give the translation in Aramaic for those who did not know Hebrew.

4. A reading from the prophets followed (Luke 4:16–21), which was also translated into Aramaic. (The Psalms were apparently not read during the synagogue service.)

5. When a capable person was available, he was invited to expound the passage to the congregation (Luke 4:21). If a stranger were present, he was invited to give an exhortation (Acts 13:15).

6. The service concluded with a priest pronouncing the Aaronic benediction of Numbers 6:24–26. The congregation responded, "Amen."

The above service was held on the Sabbath (Saturday) morning. Other services were held daily in larger towns, while the regular Monday and Thursday services were abbreviated from the above.

The synagogue greatly impacted the Jewish community both in worship and in education. It is also apparent that Christians adapted their form of worship largely from the Jewish synagogue.

## PHARISEES

### *Meaning and Origin*

The name *Pharisees* means "separated" and reflects the Pharisees' thinking; they considered themselves "the separated ones," the holy community of Israel. They identified with the common people and held sway over the masses. (Yet the Pharisees despised the *Am ha-arets,* the "common people" who did not know or keep the Law. The Pharisees considered them profane.) To be a Pharisee was to hold to a certain form of interpretation, but that did not mean the Pharisees were educated in the scribal tradition. While scribes were usually Pharisaic in belief, not all Pharisees were scribes; however, the influential leaders in the Pharisaic communities were scribes.

The Pharisees were a closed community of about six thousand. (The population of Jerusalem was about twenty-five thousand at this time; there were about eighteen thousand priests and Levites, and about four thousand Essenes in the land.) One could become a Pharisee only through observation of strict rules, and that only after a month or even a year of probation during which faithfulness to Pharisaism had to be demonstrated. Yet a large number of laymen joined the Pharisaic community, pledging to keep the primary Pharisaic laws of tithing and purity. As peasants, merchants, and artisans, these laymen were unlearned.

The new Pharisee was then obligated to keep the Pharisaic laws of purity and tithes (Matt. 15:1–2; 23:25–26; 23:23; Mark 7:1–4; Luke

11:39–42; 18:12). These two points were important to the Pharisees.

### Beliefs and Teachings

*The Law.* The Pharisees were legalistic, having codified the Mosaic Law into 365 prohibitions and 248 positive commands. Adherents to Pharisaism were bound to keep these 613 commandments. Through their elaborate system of laws, the Pharisees placed heavy burdens on the people (Matt. 23:4).

*Laws of Purity and Tithing.* This was the essence of Pharisaism. They developed elaborate laws on purity. For example, they instructed the way hands were to be washed, how they were to be held if they were dirty, how they were to be rubbed, and finally, if the water did not extend to the wrist, the hands were not considered washed!

Any legalistic system—not just the ancient Pharisees—can bring people under bondage. Jesus sets us free from legalism and bondage to an external system. Meditate on Matthew 11:28–30. How does Jesus free us from the burden of legalism?

In tithing, Pharisees were meticulous—as well as ostentatious. They tithed the tiniest seeds and drew the condemnation of Jesus because they omitted weightier matters (Matt. 23:23). But they loved the public recognition when they paid their tithes. In the Court of Women in the Temple were thirteen trumpet-shaped offering receptacles that descended to a specifically designated offering chest. When coins were deposited, a trumpetlike noise sounded as the coin descended through the trumpet-shaped cone to the chest. Jesus denounced this public display of giving (Matt. 6:1–2).

*Prayer.* Pharisees developed elaborate interpretations and teachings, including fixed times for prayer. A basic trait of the Pharisee was to recite the *Shema* in the morning and in the evening, followed by reciting the "Eighteen Benedictions." They also loved to pray in public places—at street corners or at the entrance of the synagogue to be seen as pious people (Matt. 6:5; Luke 18:9–14).

*Fasting.* Pharisees prescribed Monday and Thursday as days of fasting; and to ensure that people observed them fasting, the Pharisees blackened their faces, put ashes on their head, wore old clothing, refused to wash or anoint themselves, or trim their beards (Matt. 6:16).

*Eternal Life and Punishment.* Pharisees believed in life after death. They taught "that all souls are incorruptible; but that the souls of good men are only removed into other bodies,—but that the souls of bad men are subject to eternal punishment" (Josephus, *Wars of the Jews*, 2.8.14). They further taught "that under the earth there will be rewards or punishments, according as they have lived virtuously or viciously in this life; and the latter are to be detained in an everlasting prison, but that the former shall have power to revive and live again" (Josephus, *Antiquities*, 18.1.3). They based this belief on Daniel 12:1–2.

The Pharisees developed elaborate details concerning the resurrection; they speculated, for example, about the clothes in which one would rise. Some taught they would rise in precisely the same clothes in which they were buried; another taught that as a grain of wheat was buried naked but rose clothed, so would people. But for the pious a special resurrection was prepared. The Pharisees taught there were underground cavities in which the bodies of the righteous would roll to Israel and rise in Israel in the resurrection!

Sadducees denied life after death and eternal rewards and punishment in Hades (Josephus, *Wars of the Jews*, 2.8.14). Sadducees believed

The Pharisees had developed elaborate rituals—even for so common a thing as hand washing. For hands to be considered "washed," the Pharisees prescribed the following: "The water was poured on both hands, which must be free of anything covering them, such as gravel, mortar, etc. The hands were lifted up, so as to make the water run to the wrist, in order to ensure that the whole hand was washed, and that the water polluted by the hand did not again run down the fingers. Similarly, each hand was rubbed with the other (the fist), provided the hand that rubbed had been affused: otherwise, the rubbing might be done against the head, or even against a wall. . . . If the water remained short of the wrist . . . the hands were not clean. . . . If the hands were 'defiled,' two affusions were required: . . . On the affusion of the first waters the hands were elevated, and the water made to run down to the wrist, while at the second waters the hands were depressed, so that the water might run off by the finger points and tips" (Alfred Edersheim, *The Life and Times of Jesus the Messiah*, 2:11–12).

How can believers strike the balance between carefully observing the teachings of Scripture without becoming legalistic or prideful? What can we learn and how can we apply Jesus' instruction in Luke 11:39–44?

The Talmud cites seven kinds of Pharisees.

"that souls die with the bodies" (Josephus, *Antiquities of the Jews*, 18.1.4).

*Angels.* Pharisees also believed in angels and spirits, developing elaborate teachings by structuring angels into hierarchies as well as personalizing them. Apparently this teaching had Babylonian and Persian origins. The Sadducees objected to this Pharisaic teaching.

*Sovereignty of God and Human Freedom.* Pharisees "ascribe all to fate (or providence) and to God, and yet allow, that to act what is right, or the contrary, is principally in the power of men, although fate does co-operate in every action" (Josephus, *Wars of the Jews*, 2.8.14). Pharisees acknowledged God's sovereignty, but "they do not take away the freedom from men of acting as they think fit" (Josephus, *Antiquities of the Jews*, 18.1.3). As a Pharisee, Josephus attempted to cast them in a favorable light; however, Pharisees actually carried the doctrine of God's sovereignty to fatalism. Contrarily, Sadducees said "that to act what is good, or what is evil, is at men's own choice" (Josephus, *Wars of the Jews*, 2.8.14).

## SCRIBES

### Meaning

During New Testament times a new upper class arose—the scribes. While the present-day term suggests a secretary, the ancient scribe was far from being a secretary. The scribe was an interpreter of Mosaic Law, rendering decisions and judging legal cases. In New Testament times he was in authority and social position equivalent to the Old Testament prophet, particularly because he had the "secret teachings of God."

## Background and Class

The origin of the scribes dates back to the time of Ezra who initiated the study and instruction of the Law (Neh. 8–10). In the next centuries the scribes developed the Law, creating interpretations and legally binding statements where the Old Testament was silent. Many of the priestly aristocracy were scribes, as well as numerous ordinary priests. But people from different classes of society also became scribes, including some merchants and artisans, including a carpenter and a tentmaker. The famous Hillel was a scribe. Among the scribes were those of pure Israelite family descent such as Paul (Rom. 11:1; Phil. 3:5), but there were also scribes who descended from proselytes of pagan origin.

## Training and Position

Unlike the Pharisees who included any who held to Pharisaic beliefs but did not necessarily have formal training, the scribes committed to intensive training. No one became a scribe without this rigorous training, which lasted several years. Training began early in life; Josephus himself became an interpreter of the Law at age fourteen. When the student had mastered the traditional studies and was able to interpret questions about the Law, he was considered a "nonordained scholar." Later—some say at age forty—he was ordained and received into the elite society of the scribes as a fully "ordained scholar." From that point the scribe made his own decisions; he could judge criminal cases and civil cases. He could be called by the title "Rabbi" (Matt. 23:7–8).

The scribes developed the traditions from the Torah (the first five books of the Old Testament), and these teachings themselves came to

The Pharisees who were members of the Sanhedrin (Supreme Court of Israel) were all scribes. Nicodemus was a scribe (John 3:1), as was Gamaliel, Paul's teacher (Acts 5:34; 22:3).

have authority equivalent to the Old Testament Scriptures—and even above the Scriptures. With their knowledge and authority, the scribes had the power to "bind or loose" in judgment (cf. Matt. 16:19; 18:18). As such they held influential positions in government and education. The scribes served in judicial capacity as both legislators and judges.

### Knowledge and Authority

The scribes became the guardians of the secret knowledge of God. They had restrictions that permitted the discussion of the story of Creation and deep secrets of God (Ezek. 1, 10) only among two scribes—and that in hushed tones, frequently with their heads covered in reverence. Prophetic truth was also denied to the majority of people. The scribes themselves developed great doctrinal treatises that were considered divinely inspired but were withheld from most people.

They also withheld teachings from the people so that the teachings would not be used incorrectly. The scribes believed that since these esoteric teachings were the "secret of God" they could only be communicated orally from teacher to pupil; it was forbidden to write down these teachings. (In the second century, however, these teachings were written down, making them accessible to all people.) For this reason Jews from all over the world came to sit at the feet of the scribes and receive their teachings. And for this reason also, the scribes were revered like the Old Testament prophets. In this capacity they served as jurists who developed the Law, as teachers of the Law, and as judges of the Law.

# ECONOMY

## FARMING AND AGRICULTURE: GRAIN

### Preparing the Soil

Because of the arid climate, the soil became hard after the long, hot summer. For this reason the farmer had to wait for the "early" rains which came in October and November to soften the soil (Ps. 65:10; Jer. 14:4).

The plough consisted of two beams, fashioned as a T, with part of the crosspiece serving as the handle for the farmer and the other end functioning as a plough. The long piece extended between two oxen or donkeys and was attached to a yoke which was fastened to the necks of the animals. Originally the plough was simply a wooden stake, but later the Philistines developed the use of copper which gave them a military advantage over the Hebrews (cf. 1 Sam. 13:19–22). After the Davidic period, Hebrews also had access to iron.

Pairs of oxen or donkeys were used to plough, but Mosaic Law forbade using two different kinds of animals (Deut. 22:10). With a goad, a long stick with a sharp point, the farmer prodded the oxen along. The goad also became a formidable weapon when Shamgar the judge killed six hundred Philistines with it (Judg. 3:31).

Because of the hardness of the soil, it was difficult for the farmer to penetrate the soil for more than several inches. For that reason the farmer had to bear down on the plough with his weight to plough a sufficiently deep furrow. If he looked back, he would slacken the plough, and it would not plow a sufficiently deep furrow (Luke 9:62).

"But Jesus told him, 'Anyone who puts a hand to the plow and then looks back is not fit for the Kingdom of God'" (Luke 9:62, NLT).

### Sowing the Seed

Wheat and barley were two major crops grown in Israel (Deut. 8:8; Ruth 2:23; 2 Sam. 17:28). Wheat was considered a more valuable crop and was grown on fertile land such as the Jezreel Valley, the Jordan Valley, and the Philistine Plain (Ps. 81:16). Barley was considered a poor person's crop and was grown on poorer soil. The dream about the barley loaf, which Gideon heard, spoke of poverty (Judg. 13).

How important is "spiritual plowing" for the Word of God to penetrate the heart and effect change? Study Matthew 13:19–23. Why do some people not respond to the Word of God? See 2 Corinthians 4:4; Galatians 1:4; Ephesians 2:2. How is this dilemma resolved?

Sowing and plowing were generally undertaken together. The seed was brought to the field in a large sack on the back of a donkey. The farmer carried a sack of grain himself which he refilled from the sack on the donkey. He would scatter the seed with his hand while another man followed him with the plough, burying the seeds to prevent the birds from snatching up the seeds (Matt. 13:4).

It was important that the seed be buried in rich soil that had depth for it to grow and mature. Footpaths sometimes ran through the farmer's field; when the seed landed on the path, it likely would not germinate because either the birds would eat it or the hardness of the soil would prevent germination (Matt. 13:4). Rocky soil was similarly hazardous for germination (Matt. 13:5). In unclean fields, inhabited by tares which looked like wheat, the germinated plants were indistinguishable in the beginning (cf. Matt. 13:24–30).

### Harvesting

The standing stalks were cut just below the heads of grain with a handheld sickle (Jer. 50:16). Originally the sickle was made of wood or even the jawbone of an animal. Later crude metal sickles were used. The grain was then bound in sheaves, loaded on the back of a donkey, and taken to the hilltop for threshing. The standing stalks became grazing food for sheep. The corners of the fields were not harvested so poor people, who followed the harvesters, might gather the standing grain for themselves (Lev. 23:22; Ruth 2:2–3).

### Threshing

Threshing was done in several ways. A small amount of grain was threshed by beating the grain with a curved stick (Ruth 2:17). In fear of the Midianites, Gideon was using this method to harvest wheat in a winepress (Judg. 6:11)! Larger amounts of grain were threshed on a flat surface on a hilltop, where the wind could readily blow the chaff away. The grain was placed on the elevated floor; oxen pulled a cart fastened to two wooden runners studded with pieces of metal or stone across the grain, causing it to separate from the chaff. The chopped straw became fodder for the cattle. Sometimes the cattle walked over grain, separating it from chaff. Cattle crushing the grain illustrates a brutal conqueror crushing his enemies (Dan. 7:23).

In two of his letters, Paul quoted Deuteronomy 25:4: "Do not muzzle an ox while it is treading out the grain." Paul was saying that Christian workers should be compensated for their labors.

### Winnowing

Since a breeze would usually blow in the evening, that was the time the grain was winnowed (Ruth 3:2). The grain and chaff—now separated by the threshing—were gathered into a large pile. With a winnowing fork, a five-pronged wooden fork, the farmer threw the grain and chaff into the air against the wind. The heavier grain fell to the ground, while the straw settled nearby and the lighter chaff was driven farther away by the wind. The straw later became fodder for the cattle, while the chaff was burned.

Psalm 1 says the ungodly are "like chaff which the wind driveth away" (v. 4, KJV).

## *Sifting*

Although the grain had been separated from the chaff, it was nonetheless unclean, containing bits of dirt, small stones, and impurities such as darnels or tares (Matt. 13:24–30). The grain was placed in a sieve and shaken back and forth by a person sitting on the ground. The grain fell to the mat on the ground while the impurities remained in the sieve.

## *Storage*

After the grain had been sifted, it was stored. Smaller quantities of grain (and flour) were stored in measured earthenware jars (1 Kings 17:12); larger quantities were stored in dry, underground cisterns or barns (Deut. 28:8; Prov. 3:10; Matt. 13:30; Luke 12:18) and even in public granaries.

## FARMING AND AGRICULTURE: OLIVES

### *Characteristics*

The olive tree has a rough bark with dull green leaves that appear silver in the sunshine. The olive itself is oblong and green in color when it is young, but it turns black when it is mature. The olive plant begins to bear fruit after seven years, and reaches maturity in fifteen years but does not reach its full potential for forty or fifty years. It produces for hundreds of years. Old trees throw new shoots that will grow into strong trees. It is not a large tree, growing only to about eighteen feet. Undoubtedly because of its value in so many ways, the olive tree appeared beautiful to the people of Israel (Jer. 11:16; Hos. 14:6).

Apparently the olive trees in the Garden of Gethsemane, while not the original trees from the time of Christ, are probably trees that have grown from the stumps of the original trees.

Growing amid rocks on hillsides, the olive tree lives very long, growing well in a climate of cool, damp winters and hot summers.

## Harvesting

Olives are harvested in September or October by women and children. A large cloth is placed under the tree, and the harvesters shake the tree and beat the branches so the olives fall to the ground. The olives that remained on the tree were left for the poor (Deut. 24:20; Isa. 17:6).

## The Olive Press

Near the olive grove the farmer had an olive press, a huge wheel that would crush the olives, producing the pulp which was pressed to extract the rich oil. Extracting the oil from the pulp was done by putting the pulp in two baskets and squeezing them together by a wood beam. Sometimes the pulp was placed in cloth bags and squeezed by stepping on the bags; the oil seeped through the bags.

The oil was poured into jars and the sediment allowed to settle. Then the oil was drained into jars and kept in a cool location.

## Use

The olive is a highly useful product in the land of Israel. It is a primary food that is eaten (with barley bread, it constituted a normal breakfast) fried and over salads, used for olive oil and as butter (Deut. 7:13; 2 Kings 4:5; 2 Chron 2:10; Ezek. 16:13). Since olives could be preserved in salt water, the availability of this important food product could be extended.

Olives were also used in making soap. Olive oil was further used for personal purposes for grooming and rubbing on the skin after bathing, making the skin and head shiny (Ruth 3:3;

1 Kings 1:34; Ps. 23:5; Luke 7:46). To anoint the feet of a guest was to bestow honor on the guest (Luke 7:46; John 12:3). Corpses were also anointed (Mark 16:1; Luke 23:56; John 19:39). Olives were used for medicinal purposes (Isa. 1:6; Mark 6:13; James 5:14). Olive oil was also used as fuel for lamps (Exod. 25:6; Matt. 25:3–4). Olive oil was even used as a laxative. The cherubim in the inner sanctuary in Solomon's Temple were carved from olive wood (1 Kings 6:23). The doors entering the sanctuary were olive wood, with ornately carved cherubim, palm trees, and flowers (1 Kings 6:32).

Prophets (1 Kings 19:16), priests (Exod. 30:30; Lev. 8:12), and kings (1 Sam. 10:1; 16:13; 1 Kings 1:34; 19:15–16) were all anointed with olive oil, inducting them into their God-ordained offices. It is evident that olive oil was very valuable for many reasons.

### Symbolic Meaning

The olive is frequently used to denote the peaceful conditions in the land; conversely, its absence infers the judgment of God upon the land (Amos 4:9; Mic. 6:15). The olive plant pictured a fruitful family, numerous children like olive plants around the table (Ps. 128:3–4). In contrast to the wicked, the righteous man is pictured like a fruitful olive tree in the house of God (Ps. 52:8). When Israel was about to enter the Promised Land, the land was described as "a land of olive oil," suggesting the fruitful productivity of the land (Deut. 8:8).

### FARMING AND AGRICULTURE: FIGS

### Description

Fig trees are common in Israel, growing to a height of thirty feet (Num. 13:23; Deut. 8:8). They were valuable for their fruit. The early figs

**Messiah**

Both the Hebrew word *Mashiah* and the Greek word *Christos* mean "the Anointed One" and point to the Messiah; He is the Anointed One of God. The anointing of the prophets, priests, and kings pointed forward to Jesus, who would be the ultimate Anointed One of God, the Messiah. He would combine in His one person the offices of prophet, priest, and king (cf. Isa. 61:1; Luke 4:17–21).

could be eaten a month before the main crop. The normal crop ripened in August and September, while the winter figs stayed on the trees until late fall.

The fruit of a fig tree appeared before the leaves; hence, when there were leaves on a fig tree, it was an indication there was fruit. It would have had some old figs from the previous year, but it would also have had new figs, and though unripe, they were often eaten by hungry travelers. Both the Mishnah and the Talmud suggest the unripe figs were eaten as soon as they assumed a reddish color. When Christ saw that the fig tree had leaves but no fruit, He cursed it, symbolizing impending judgment on the nation Israel (Matt. 21:18–21). The tree was making an empty profession; by its leaves it claimed to have fruit, but it had none.

The fig tree also at times symbolized Israel. When Christ came as the nation's Messiah, the nation made an empty profession, symbolized by the fig tree (Matt. 21:18–21). The fig tree does *not always* represent Israel. In Matthew 24:32, Christ used a simple illustration. When the fig tree puts out leaves (April), summer is near. Similarly, when the signs of the tribulation take place, Christ's coming is near (Matt. 24:32–33). To suggest the fig tree represents Israel in this parable has led to many false interpretations.

### Use

Figs were commonly eaten fresh, but they were also dried on the rooftops, then eaten throughout the year. Figs were also used to make cakes (1 Sam. 25:18; 30:12; 1 Chron. 12:40). Additionally, figs were used medically; when Hezekiah was sick, he was given a poultice of

The fig tree symbolized prosperity in Israel. The expression "every man under his vine and his fig tree, from Dan even to Beersheba" (1 Kings 4:25, NASB) indicated the people were enjoying affluence throughout the land. This figure is also used to describe the peaceful, prosperous conditions in the millennial kingdom (Mic. 4:4; Zech. 3:10).

figs, which was an ancient remedy for healing boils (2 Kings 20:7).

## SHEPHERD

Shepherding was a prominent occupation in Israel, beginning with Abel (Gen. 4:2). Abraham (Gen. 12:16), Jacob (Gen. 30:31–40), and Moses (Exod. 3:1) were all shepherds. Since older men were useful for physically demanding work such as farming, shepherding usually fell to the youngest son in the family. When Samuel inquired about Jesse's sons, David, the youngest, was away shepherding the sheep (1 Sam. 16:11–12).

### Instruments

Since the shepherd protected the sheep from both animal predators and robbers and also sought the straying sheep, several instruments were vital to the shepherd's task.

*Club.* The club or "rod" is mentioned in Psalm 23:4. It was a heavy weapon, usually with a large knot on the end, sometimes embedded with nails. With the rod the shepherd protected the sheep from wild animals. David killed a lion and bear—probably with the aid of his club (1 Sam. 17:34–36). The rod was also used for counting the sheep, separating every tenth animal (Ezek. 20:37). Here the club is also seen as disciplinary, figurative of disciplining Israel in the tribulation but later bringing the nation safely into the Promised Land (Ezek. 20:37–39).

In counting the sheep, the end of the staff was dipped in dye; when the sheep passed under the rod or staff, every tenth sheep was marked with dye and given to the Lord as the tithe (Lev. 27:31–33).

*Staff.* The shepherd's staff was a six-foot-long stick, sometimes curved at the end, and used for snaring the straying sheep (Ps. 23:4). It aided the shepherd in walking over rugged terrain. The shepherd also used the staff to count and guide the sheep into the sheepfold at night.

*Scrip.* The shepherd's scrip was a leather pouch where he kept his lunch. The shepherd took fresh goat's milk in his pouch in the morning; and in walking the hot hills of Israel, by the time he ate, the milk had turned to curds—much like yogurt (Isa. 7:15, 22). Curds were sometimes eaten with honey (Isa. 7:22). The scrip (perhaps a different one) was where David kept the stones he used in his battle with Goliath (1 Sam. 17:40).

*Sling.* The sling had two strands of rope and a pouch where a stone was held. Twirling the sling over his head several times, the shepherd let go of one of the strands, hurling the rock at its object. Its forcefulness is evident in the slaying of Goliath (1 Sam. 17:49). The shepherd also released stones toward straying sheep, dropping the stones near the sheep causing them to return to the fold.

*Flute or Pipe.* The shepherd had a flute or pipe, made of two hollow pieces of cane. David may have played a flute when he composed psalms.

### Duties

*Grazing the Sheep.* It was the shepherd's responsibility to provide food and water for the sheep. Because of the desert conditions of much of Israel, the shepherd constantly sought for green pastures, moving the sheep to suitable grazing (Ps. 23:2a).

Because sheep are easily frightened, the shepherd sought a quiet, gently flowing stream to water the sheep (Ps. 23:2b; cf. 36:8). When a stream was unavailable, the shepherd sought a well (Gen. 29:8–10).

*Restoring Straying Sheep.* Since sheep are helpless, it was particularly important for the shepherd to watch for straying sheep and to restore them to the fold. Humanity is frequently pictured as sinful, straying sheep (Isa. 53:6) with the Lord, the true Shepherd, restoring the sheep (Ps. 23:3; Luke 15:6).

In John 10:1–18, Jesus described Himself as the Good Shepherd. What response does this call forth from Jesus' followers?

*Protecting in the Sheepfold.* In the evening the shepherd brought the sheep into the sheepfold, which was a square, stone enclosure. Sometimes the shepherd quickly made a temporary sheepfold out of thorn bushes. A cave also served as a sheepfold, with a partial stone wall built across the entrance.

*Guiding Them to Pasture.* The shepherd walked ahead of the sheep, leading them to pasture (cf. John 10:4). The sheep followed the shepherd because they recognized his voice. Even when several flocks of sheep became intermingled, when the shepherd called his sheep and began walking, his sheep followed him; they recognized his voice (John 10:4, 27). In larger flocks dogs would follow the sheep, bringing the straying sheep back to the fold (Job 30:1).

## FISHING

In New Testament times there were numerous cities encircling the Sea of Galilee, prospering from the fishing industry. The Israelites did not major on deep-sea fishing in the Mediterranean, nor did they fish in the Dead Sea, since it contains no fish apart from the mouth where the Jordan empties into the Dead Sea. Fishing was done in a variety of ways.

### Line and Hook

Isaiah 19:8, NASB, mentions those who "cast a line into the Nile." Job rhetorically asked, "Can you draw out Leviathan [a crocodile] with a fishhook?" (41:1, NASB)—implying that people were fishing with hooks in the Nile River. In the New Testament the fishhook is mentioned only once when used literally. To show that He paid taxes, Jesus instructed Peter to "throw in a hook, and take the first fish that comes up" (Matt. 17:27, NASB). The fish would have the needed coin in its mouth—sufficient to pay Jesus' and Peter's tax. This may have been the *clarias macracanthus,* popularly called "St. Peter's fish," which was large enough to have a coin in its mouth.

### Spear

Job mentioned two different words for spear fishing: "harpoons" and "fishing spears" (Job 41:7). Although Job mentioned the spear in men's hunting the crocodile, spearfishing was also common for fishing in shallow water.

### Hand Net

The hand net was a circular net with weights on the outside and lines from the outside to an opening in the middle. As the fisherman threw the net flat on the lake, the weights drew the net to the bottom, drawing in the lines from the circumference and trapping the fish inside the net. Peter and Andrew were casting hand nets when Jesus called them (Matt. 4:18).

### Drag Net

The dragnet was similar to the modern seine net; it was about eight feet wide and several hundred feet long. It was suspended vertically in the water with weights at one end, drawing the net into the water, and corks at the other end for floatation. The net was launched from two boats with the boats forming a circle and drawing the net to shore (Luke 5:4). Numerous fish of all kinds were caught in the net. After use, the nets were washed (Luke 5:2) and mended (Matt. 4:21, NASB).

Have you ever wondered where the fish symbol, designating a Christian, comes from? The Greek word for fish is *ichthus,* five letters in the Greek alphabet. When each of the letters is used for a Greek word, it can spell the following: *Iesus* = Jesus; *Christos* = Christ; *Theos* = God; *Uios* = Son; *Soterion* = Savior; hence, it spells "Jesus Christ, God's Son [our] Savior. It portrayed belief in Jesus Christ. This Christian symbol may have begun in the catacombs of Rome when persecution of Christians was fierce.

In Matthew 13:47–50, Jesus used dragnet fishing to illustrate the end of the age.

## HUNTING

From the beginning of recorded history, men were hunters. Nimrod was "a mighty hunter before the LORD" (Gen. 10:9). Ishmael became an "archer" (Gen. 21:20). The Hebrew text uses two words, first a general word and then a more specific word, "an archer, a bowsman" to describe Ishmael's prowess as a hunter in the desert. Of Esau the text is more descriptive, identifying Jacob's brother as a hunter (Gen. 27:3–4). In addition to deer, the gazelle was also hunted for food (Deut. 12:15).

Hunting was a prominent method of providing food for the home. Men not only hunted large animals, like deer, but also birds. Quail were plentiful in the desert, providing food for the Israelites as they journeyed to the Promised Land (Exod. 16:13; Num. 11:31–32). Birds were killed by a trap or net or with a bow and arrow.

Hunting was essential not only for food but also to protect the sheep from predatory animals such as lions, leopards, bears, wolves, and hyenas. As a shepherd, David protected the flock from lions and bears (1 Sam. 17:34–36). Hunting was also necessary for self-protection (1 Kings 13:26–28; Amos 5:19).

In pursuing ferocious animals, pits were used. The hunters dug a pit in the ground and covered it with branches and leaves. At times the animal was even "coaxed" toward the pit. Once the animal fell into the pit, it was trapped (cf. Ezek. 19:3–4). Antelope were sometimes captured with a net (Isa. 51:20). Also commonly used in hunting were the bow and arrow as well as slingshots and javelins (Job 41:28–29). Snares were used in capturing birds (Ps. 124:7).

Mosaic Law made provision for hunting as a means of obtaining food (Lev. 17:13), but it also restricted what could be eaten (Lev. 11).

## VINEGROWERS

Vineyards were frequently planted on a hill since it wasn't useful for other forms of agriculture (Ps. 80:8–10; Jer. 31:5), but vineyards were also planted on the plain. On hillsides it was necessary to terrace the vineyard. Stones were removed from the land to make the vine more productive. A protective wall was built around the vineyard, and a tower was built in the middle of the vineyard for watchmen to guard the vineyard against marauding animals and thieves (Song of Sol. 2:15; Jer. 49:9). Foxes were notorious for ruining vineyards in blossom (Song of Sol. 2:15). The watchman lived in a hut in the vineyard during the growing season to protect the crop (Isa. 1:8). A winepress was built in the vineyard in anticipation of the grape harvest (Isa. 5:1–2; Matt. 21:33ff.).

To produce a better harvest of grapes, the landowner placed stones under the vine, raising it off the ground. (Note: The word translated "take away" in John 15:2, NASB, is the Greek verb *aireo,* which may also be translated "raise up" which seems to be the better translation.) Travelers to Israel will see the vineyards with stones propped under the vines, lifting them four to six inches off the ground.

Pruning was also essential for producing stronger vines and therefore better crops (John 15:2). By itself, the vine was unproductive, but through pruning, fruitless branches would be removed to enhance the harvest of grapes (Isa. 18:5).

The winepress was used for making wine from grapes. Cut out of the rock, the winepress had two levels, an upper and a lower level. Bunches of grapes were placed into the upper level vat where the workers would tread barefoot on the grapes amid joyful singing (Amos 9:13). The grape harvest, beginning in September, was always a time of joyful celebration (Judg. 9:27). When the grapes were crushed, the juice would run from the upper vat to a lower vat where the juice would gather. Some grape juice was made into a syrup frequently called "honey" in the Bible.

Since water was often impure, wine was an important beverage. This was the reason for Paul's instruction to Timothy (1 Tim. 5:23). Wine was a mixture of several parts of water to one part of wine; drinking wine full strength was considered barbarian. Wine was sometimes used as a disinfectant to clean wounds (Luke 10:34). Wine was also mixed with gall to relieve pain (Matt. 27:34).

Jesus used the picture of a vineyard to represent His relationship with disciples: "Remain in me, and I will remain in you. No branch can bear fruit by itself; it must remain in the vine. Neither can you bear fruit unless you remain in me" (John 15:4).

Although wine was stored in clay jars, it was also frequently stored in animal skins. When new wine was poured into a wine skin, the skin would stretch with the fermentation; when a stretched wine skin was again used to hold new wine, the wine skin would burst because its elasticity was gone (Matt. 9:17).

Fresh grapes were an important food, eaten along with bread (Deut. 23:24). To produce raisins, grapes were also dried in a corner of the vineyard. They were turned over and sprinkled with olive oil to keep them moist.

## PHYSICIANS

Physicians are not frequently mentioned in the Bible. In the New Testament they largely go unnoticed apart from Luke "the beloved physician" (Col. 4:14). See expanded discussion under "Medicine."

## TANNING, DYEING, AND WEAVING

Goatskins were valuable in providing liquid containers. Goats were skinned, with the leg and tail openings sewn up, while the neck opening became the mouth of the "bottle." Sheepskins and goatskins (the latter was considered superior) were also used for sandals.

Dyeing was a family business, and the formulas were kept secret. The effectiveness of dyeing was related to the material that was dyed. Wool, the easiest to dye, was dyed in various colors, including white, yellow, and brown. Cotton was also easy to dye; but linen, which was used in the temple, was more difficult (2 Chron. 2:7; cf. Exod. 35:6). Silk and leather were also dyed.

Ancients made a brilliant crimson dye from insects (Isa. 1:18). A more common dye was extracted from the madder plant. The rind of a pomegranate resulted in an indigo dye. The purple dye, extracted from the mollusks Purpura and Murex, symbolized wealth and status (cf. Luke 16:19). Lydia must have been a wealthy businesswoman since she was a "seller of purple fabrics" (Acts 16:14). Yellow was extracted from the safflower.

Weaving was an important and ancient craft. As early as 2000 B.C., weaving was known in Egypt. Canaanites employed this craft even before the Hebrews entered Canaan. Weaving became valuable for the Hebrews both concerning their personal clothing needs as well as for

Note Acts 10:6, and consider the progress of Peter. He was staying with "a certain tanner named Simon" (NASB). Working with carcasses, Simon the tanner would have been considered unclean. Legalistic Jews would have scorned him and refrained from any commerce with him. Yet Peter stayed in his home.

The rabbis taught: "Excellent is the study of the law together with worldly occupation, for toil in them both puts sin out of mind" (M. Aboth 2.2).

decorating the tabernacle (Exod. 26) and for priests' clothing (Exod. 28:39).

At first the horizontal loom was used; later the upright loom, pegged in the ground, was deemed more useful. Weaving involved the interlacing of threads, the warp, with other threads, called the weft. The warp threads were stretched taut on the loom with the weft threads threading over and under the warp threads. Wool, cotton, goat hair, and silk were all used in weaving. Through weaving, families produced their own clothing.

## TENTMAKERS

Since it was considered improper for a rabbi or scribe to receive remuneration for teaching, it was incumbent on a scribe to learn a trade—especially so since priests in Jesus' day served in the Temple for only two weeks in the year. Apart from that they were gainfully engaged in a trade or business.

Examine 2 Timothy 2:15, and study the phrase "accurately handling" (NASB) ("rightly dividing," KJV). This phrase means to lay out a road in a straight line or a stone mason to cut the block accurately, or perhaps from Paul's own occupation, to cut the cloth straight. What is the point of this metaphor?

Paul was trained in the trade of tent making (Acts 18:1–3). Actually, the word translated "tent making" (Gk. *skenopoios* ) may mean "tent-maker" or "leather worker." Leather materials were in demand for a variety of uses: they were used by people traveling such as soldiers, ship passengers, and visitors to the Isthmian Games. Leather was also used for awnings, walkway coverings, a shield from the sun in homes and public buildings, and for coats, flasks, and tents.

Originally tents were made from goatskins; later they were made from goat hair. The leather was produced by skinning the animal, removing the hair, scraping and applying lime, and soaking the skin in water and rubbing with dog's dung. The odor was intensely offensive, and the leather worker had to work outdoors because of it.

## CARPENTRY

Carpentry was prominent in both Egypt and Israel. The Egyptians built many products out of wood: tables, chairs, doors, and coffins. They also built chariots and carriages for travel on land and ships for navigating on water. Hebrews, too, built many products of wood. Although Hebrew skill in woodworking was limited in the beginning of their history, they received help in construction when David built Jerusalem (1 Chron. 14:1). Later, Israelites developed greater ability in construction so that Nebuchadnezzar took the skilled Hebrew workers to exile in Babylon.

Carpentry was a trade that demanded both physical strength and skill. A carpenter built everything from houses to smaller objects including plows, yokes, wooden locks, chairs, doors, roofs, windows, stools, chests, and latticework in windows. In house building, the carpenter felled trees and shaped them to produce the beams for the roof of the house—an arduous task!

Isaiah mentioned four tools of the carpenter: measuring line, marking tool (primitive pencil), plane (for scraping), and an instrument for making a circle (Isa. 44:13). The carpenter had an axe to cut trees for construction and shape the wood for building (Isa. 10:15, 34). The axe had an iron head, fastened by thongs to a wooden handle and had a tendency to slip off (Deut 19:5; 2 Kings 6:5). Nails were used (Jer. 10:4) as well as a saw (Isa. 10:15). Some axes were shaped like a chisel (Jer. 10:3).

## MASONRY

Since Israel is a land of rocks and stones, it was natural that homes would be built of stone.

While Jesus is referred to as a carpenter, the Greek word *tekton,* translated "carpenter," "has a wide range of meanings, from a shipbuilder to a sculptor, but it generally indicates a craftsman of considerable skill. The word can even be used of a physician. It seems clear that so far from Joseph being the simple—and poor—village carpenter making ox yokes or simple plows (which any peasant was capable of producing), he was probably a builder of some consequence, traveling over wide areas of country . . . our present English 'architect,' directly derived from the same Greek word, certainly does not mean a man of limited accomplishments" (W. F. Albright and C. S. Mann, "Matthew" in *The Anchor Bible,* 172–3).

"Then he show me another vision. I saw the Lord standing beside a wall that had been built using a plumb line. He was checking it with a plumb line to see if it was straight. And the LORD said to me, 'Amos, what do you see?'

"I answered, 'A plumb line.'

"And the Lord replied, 'I will test my people with this plumb line. I will no longer ignore all their sins'" (Amos 7:7–9, NLT).

Masons and stoneworkers were evident early in Israel's history. When the tabernacle was erected, God gave Bezalel divine ability in cutting and engraving stones (Exod. 35:33). When David established Jerusalem as the capital, Hiram, king of Tyre, sent stonemasons to David (2 Sam. 5:11). Egyptians, too, revealed their unusual ability in stonework in constructing the pyramids, which are to this day monuments to Egypt's magnificent prowess in building construction. Egyptians transported smaller stones on ships and rafts along the Nile River; on land they were transported by sledges and rollers.

The stonemason began construction by digging a deep trench and filling it with rock and lime and constructing a modest building on this foundation (Luke 6:48). In advanced construction, a large square cornerstone was placed at each corner where the walls were designed to meet. The cornerstone was designed to give direction to the building. There was also a thinner cornerstone on top of the walls at each corner. The beams rested on these cornerstones. The cornerstone was the most significant stone in the building (1 Cor. 3:11).

To construct a straight wall the mason used a plumb line, a weight attached to a cord, which provided a guide for building a properly perpendicular wall. When suspended alongside the wall, it revealed whether the wall was straight.

## POTTERY

Pottery is ancient—beginning as early as 5000 B.C. Potsherds (fragments of pottery) are valuable in both dating eras and providing information about life in different civilizations.

Visitors to Bethlehem today can see a potter making vessels on a potter's bench much like they did in biblical times. The potter's instrument consisted of two wheels, both lying horizontal. From the center of the bottom wheel, which was at foot level, an axle extended to the top wheel. The bottom wheel was turned by foot, simultaneously turning the top wheel. From a workbench nearby the potter took some clay, placed it on the top wheel, and began to turn the wheel with his foot. As the wheel turned around, the potter shaped the clay into the vessel he desired to make. With his thumb he fashioned a hole in the vessel until he could extend his hand into the vessel. The potter sprinkled the clay with water to maintain the proper texture. If the clay vessel was unacceptable to the potter, he simply crushed it with his hand and began again (Jer. 18:4; cf. Rom. 9:20–21). When the pot was finished, he set it aside to dry. After it had dried, the pot was hand painted or scratched with a design. Sometimes pieces of clay were attached in a design.

What does the illustration about pottery in Ecclesiastes 12:6 teach about the brevity of life? What applications can you draw?

In addition to the wheel, wooden moulds were also used in making seals (Job 38:14), oil lamps, and ornaments.

After the clay jar had dried, it was fired in a clay oven or kiln. These clay vessels tended to be brittle. Brittle pottery illustrates the total destruction of man's culture when Messiah returns to rule (Ps. 2:9; Rev. 2:27). But even the broken pieces of clay, called potsherds, were useful. Job used a potsherd to scrape his sores (Job 2:8). Potsherds were also used for carrying live coals or water (Isa. 30:14) or other objects; they were also used for writing, called *ostraca*.

Pottery was valuable and useful for many things. The potter made jars for water (Gen. 24:14), pots for meat (Exod. 16:3), bowls and jars for oil and flour (1 Kings 17:14; Isa. 22:24), cups for drinking (Song of Sol. 7:2), and pitchers for beverages (Jer. 35:5).

## METAL WORKING

Metal craftsmen appeared very early in history. With Tubal-cain emerged a civilization that made implements of bronze and iron (Gen. 4:22). This craft probably ceased with the Flood.

### *Blacksmithing*

Ironwork surfaced again during the reign of Saul (1050–1010 B.C.), but the Philistines had a monopoly on iron (1 Sam. 13:19–22). They had a military advantage over the Israelites by keeping metallurgy from them, preventing the Israelites from producing weapons of war. Later, during the days of Isaiah (ca. 740–680 B.C.), blacksmiths and metalworkers were found in Israel. Isaiah described the smiths that fashioned idols at the anvil (Isa. 41:7) and the blacksmith that fashioned tools at his forge (Isa. 44:12). Bellows were also in use to fan the flames (Jer. 6:29).

### *Coppersmithing*

The land of Israel was rich in iron and copper (Deut. 8:9). These minerals were especially mined in the desert, the Arabah, between the Dead Sea and the Gulf of Aqaba. During Solomon's reign copper mining and smelting took place near Ezion-geber, the port on the Gulf of Aqaba where metal and other products were produced and exported (1 Kings 9:26–28). The coppersmith extracted the copper from the ore by smelting; then, when the copper was pliable, it was hardened and shaped by cold hammering. By adding a small portion of tin, the copper became harder and stronger and was known as bronze. The metals were melted in a clay pot and then shaped.

Copper and bronze products were for warfare: swords, daggers, spear tips, and arrowheads; for peaceful purposes there were axes, chisels, bowls, and plowshares.

### Goldsmithing

Gold and silver were refined by subjecting the metals to intense heat, which removed the impurities and alloys and left the pure metal (Zech. 13:9; cf. Isa. 48:10). Goldsmiths fashioned idols of both silver and gold: some were gold plated; others were molten gold (Jer. 10:9; 51:17). Gold-plated idols were constructed of wood with nails fastening the gold and silver plating (Isa. 41:7; Jer. 10:3–4). The gold was hammered into sheets or special designs. When Nehemiah returned to the land, goldsmiths helped repair the wall around the city of Jerusalem (Neh. 3:8, 31–32). Goldsmiths and jewelers would also have made the numerous articles of jewelry denounced by Isaiah the prophet (Isa. 3:18–23).

"Two-thirds of the people in the land will be cut off and die, says the Lord. But a third will be left in the land. I will bring that group through the fire and make them pure, just as gold and silver are refined and purified by fire" (Zech. 13:8–9, NLT).

## MERCHANDISE

The marketplaces were normally near the city gate or along a busy street. (The visitor to old Jerusalem will observe the same customs today as the merchants gather outside and inside the Damascus Gate, the Jaffa Gate, and others.) When caravans arrived at a city, the marketplace would become active in buying and selling.

Bartering was a normal and enjoyable aspect of commerce. The bartering could take considerable time as seller and prospective buyer would argue over the price of a product, yet it was a normal part of business. (Tourist tips to visitors to the Middle East suggests that tourists should attempt to purchase a product for one-third of the first asking price!)

Bartering is illustrated in Proverbs 20:14, where the buyer depreciates the product but later boasts about his good purchase. Bartering is seen throughout Scripture. When Abraham sought a burial place for Sarah, he bargained with Ephron the Hittite for the cave where Sarah would be buried. Ephron wanted to sell Abraham not just the cave but the entire field. Ephron did not really want to *give* Abraham the cave and the field;he was intent on *selling* him both. Because of his love for Sarah, Abraham willingly bought the field as well—and paid a high price for it—four hundred shekels of silver (Gen. 23:1–16).

Since coinage was not in existence in early biblical history (coins appeared about 700 B.C.), business was conducted through trade and/or payment by precious metals.

## MONEY CHANGERS

When the Roman Crassus invaded the Temple, he carried away the equivalent of two and a half million pounds silver (*Life & Times of Jesus the Messiah*, 1:368)!

Money changers were important in Israel since at the pilgrimage feasts (Passover, Pentecost, Tabernacles) Jews who were visiting Jerusalem from foreign countries had to change their money into local currency when they came to present a sacrificial offering. All Jews had to pay the half-shekel tax (Exod. 30:13–15) in local currency. To accommodate the Jewish pilgrims coming from Greece, Syria, Egypt, Persia, and many other countries, the money changers set up stalls in all the country towns, enabling them to exchange their money. As the festival neared, the country stalls closed; and the money changers located in the Temple precincts. While opinions vary, the money changers fixed a charge of between one-sixth and one-third for exchanging the currency! This brought enormous wealth to the money changers. Alfred Edersheim estimates that the money changers enjoyed an annual profit of nine thousand pounds sterling, while the Temple tax realized an annual income of seventy-five thousand pounds sterling.

Since the Jewish pilgrims had to purchase many things for worship, the money changers did a brisk business. As the animal sacrifices were brought, the priests had to inspect and approve the animals, and the worshiper was charged for the inspection. Since Annas, the former high priest controlled the Temple business (called the "Bazaars of Annas"), the priests would reject as imperfect the animal the worshiper brought with him. The worshiper was then forced to buy an animal from the "Bazaars of Annas" at an inflated price and pay the money changer for exchanging the coinage. Poor people could only afford to offer pigeons as a sacrifice, but on one occasion even a pair of pigeons cost the poor worshiper a Roman gold denarius. By the time the worshiper came to offer his sacrifice, the joy of worship was gone. The priests and money changers had sufficiently gouged the worshiper and corrupted the worship of God. The Temple became a place of financial profiteering rather than worship. It is no wonder Jesus drove the money changers from the Temple (John 2:13–17).

## TAX COLLECTORS

Under Roman rule in the New Testament, tax collection was farmed out to local people. Rome demanded a certain amount of money in taxes, and the highest bidder purchased the right to collect the money for Rome. There were no limitations concerning the amount the tax collector

"There was a tax and duty upon all imports and exports; on all that was bought and sold; bridge money, road money, harbor dues, town dues, etc. The classical reader knows the ingenuity which could invent a tax and find a name for every kind of exaction, such as on axles, wheels, pack animals, pedestrians, roads, highways; on admission to markets; on carriers, bridges, ships, and quays; on crossing rivers, on dams, on licenses—in short, on such a variety of objects that even the research of modern scholars has not been able to identify all the names" (Merrill F. Unger, *The New Unger's Bible Dictionary*, 1255).

"Then Jesus entered the Temple and began to drive out the merchants from their stalls. He told them, 'The Scriptures declare, "My Temple will be a place of prayer," but you have turned it into a den of thieves'" (Luke 19:45–46, NLT).

could add to the taxes for his own profit, so the tax collectors usually added an excessive—and burdensome—amount to be collected for Rome. As a result, the tax collectors—although they were fellow Jews—became despised and classified with harlots and sinners (Matt. 9:11; 21:31; Luke 15:1). These fellow Jews were considered traitors to their nation, having sold out to Rome, the foreign occupying power.

Consider further the impact of Luke 19:8. Money makes people (even Christians) do strange things. How should we expect Christ to transform us regarding our money? Note also how Christ transformed Levi, another tax collector, so that he was burdened for the salvation of his friends and gave an evangelistic banquet (Luke 5:27). See also Luke 18:9–14.

The tax collectors set up stations on the main roads (as well as at harbors) where the caravans traveled; and upon entering the country, the tax collectors examined the goods being transported and assessed a tax on the traveler more or less indiscriminately. In addition to the taxes the traveler had to pay, it was annoying to be interrupted on the journey, having to unload the pack animals and open every package to the scrutiny of the ruthless tax collector. He could do it; he had the power of Rome behind him. The excessive taxation is evident since John the Baptist admonished the tax collectors: "Collect no more than what you have been ordered to" (Luke 3:13, NASB).

Zacchaeus is the only one in Scripture termed "a chief tax collector" (Luke 19:2). Zacchaeus employed local tax collectors who worked under him to collect taxes. Zacchaeus was probably in charge of the toll taxes for goods passing from Perea to Judea. As a result, Zacchaeus became a rich man.

# CITIES AND TOWNS

Towns and cities were distinguished from villages because they had walls while villages had none (Lev. 25:29, 31). Villages were located near towns and cities to come under the umbrella of the city's protection. Cities are frequently identified with villages; in the allocation of Israel's territory in Canaan, the cities are listed and the unnamed surrounding villages are included (cf. Josh. 15:32, 36, 41, etc.). Cities and towns were small, averaging five to ten acres.

## WALLS

Walls were important for the protection of the city (2 Chron. 32:5). When Nehemiah returned to Jerusalem from captivity in Babylon, a major concern was rebuilding the wall for protection against Israel's enemies. As long as the Jerusalem's wall was broken down, the city was vulnerable to attack by its enemies (Neh. 1:3). When Nehemiah began to rebuild the wall, Israel's enemies were furious; they knew the city would become defensible once the walls were built (Neh. 4:13).

Cities were normally built on a hill, making an attack on the city more difficult. With the foundation wall made of stone and the wall itself made of brick, the wall tended to follow the contour of the hill on which the city was built, so that any approach to the city was uphill. With the protective wall surrounding the city, the attackers had to breach the walls with an uphill assault—a military difficulty. Even the city of Jericho—which was only eight acres in size—was defensible against the Israelites (Josh. 6:1). Surrounding Jericho was both an inner

"The wealth of the rich is their fortified city; they imagine it an unscalable wall" (Prov. 18:11).

wall, twelve feet thick and thirty feet high, and an outer wall, six feet thick and twelve feet high. The approach to the city was a difficult a thirty-five degree incline. Between the two series of walls was a rampart of stone and debris fill, covered with limestone. If Jericho were going to fall, it would have to be supernatural!

When a city was destroyed, the rubble was leveled, and the invaders built a new city on top of the old. With time and successive destructions, the city level rose. Archaeologists can determine the culture of the people occupying a city by the different occupation levels when they slice through the existing hill.

The ancient city of Babylon had an outer wall, eleven feet thick, and an inner wall, twenty-one feet thick, with a tower every sixty feet. Nebuchadnezzar expanded the length of the outer wall to seventeen miles, enclosing his summer palace and the plain. Later writers indicate a middle wall that reached three hundred feet in height, with 420 foot towers.

## GATES

The doors of the city gates were two halves, constructed of wood and covered with bronze and protected with iron bars (Ps. 107:16; 1 Sam. 23:7; Isa. 45:2). The keys for the locks on the city gates were large, as much as two feet in length (Isa. 22:22). Later, for added protection, a series of gates was built with a courtyard separating the gates.

The city gate was important for many reasons. The marketplace with its boisterous bartering was located at the city gate (2 Kings 7:1, 18; Prov. 1:21). The civic court, with the elders of the city, was also located at the city gate (Job 29:7; Prov. 31:23). When Boaz proposed to marry Ruth and become her kins-man-redeemer, he brought the matter to the city elders and the people at the city gate (Ruth 4:9–12). At the city gate the manslayer had an opportunity to present his case to the city officials before being permitted residency (Josh. 20:4). Lot, Abraham's nephew, sat in the gate of Sodom, indicating he had an influential civic position in the sinful city (Gen. 19:1).

The city gate was also the gathering place for important announcements and the dissemination of information (2 Chron. 32:6). Hamor discussed Jacob's sons' proposal with his people at the city gate (Gen. 34:20). David sensed the people at the gate whispering about him (Ps. 69:12). Ezra the scribe read the Word of God in the presence of the people gathered at the Water Gate in Jerusalem (Neh. 8:1, 3). Prophets frequently proclaimed God's Word to the people at the city gate (Jer. 7:2; 17:19).

Read Psalm 61:3: "For you have been my refuge, a strong tower against the foe." What does this image communicate about God? What is the appropriate response to this truth?

Towers were also built beside the city gate, permitting the city's defenders to pour hot liquids and throw heavy objects at the city's attackers. When Abimelech attacked the tower at Thebez, "a certain woman threw an upper millstone on Abimelech's head, crushing his skull" (Judg. 9:53). The tower also served as the watchman's lookout in defense of the city (cf. 2 Sam. 18:24–26). The watchman would be stationed at the tower where he could see a long distance across the landscape (cf. Jer. 6:17; Ezek. 3:17). Towers were also built at the corners of the city wall where the defenders could shoot arrows and hurl stones at the invaders (2 Chron. 26:15).

Read Revelation 21:21 (NLT): "The twelve gates were made of pearls—each gate from a single pearl! And the main street was pure gold, as clear as glass." What is the point of contrast in the street of the New Jerusalem with the old Jerusalem?

## MARKETPLACES

(Note: "Marketplace" was covered under "Food and Meals.")

## STREETS

Streets were narrow, more like alleys, with houses and buildings constructed right up to the street. Other narrow streets ran off the main streets to gain access to houses (Prov. 7:8). Normally streets ran from a main plaza in the town. Household wastes and debris were thrown into the street, which being unpaved, became muddy and filthy (Ps. 18:42; Isa. 10:6). Roman streets tended to be wide, straight, and paved. Romans also provided drainage below the streets that carried the sewage away.

On Straight Street in Damascus, Paul stayed at the house of a man named Judas. At this house, Ananias was instrumental in Paul's conversion and introduction into the Christian fellowship (Acts 9:11). A narrow street by this name exists today in Damascus, Syria.

## WATER

Because of the lack of rain during the long summer, water was critical. It was the important lifeline in a community; hence, towns were frequently built near a water supply. Lot chose to live near Sodom and Gomorrah because it was well watered (Gen. 13:10). Jericho, one of oldest cities in the world, was built near a spring. At other times wells were dug to obtain water and even became the point of contention (Gen. 21:22–34; 26:18–22). In the arid climate, a water supply was important both for human existence and for maintaining herds and flocks (Gen. 29:2–3). The well in Samaria where Jesus stopped to rest and asked the Samaritan woman for a drink of water (John 4:6–7) remains in existence to this day. Visitors to Jerusalem can walk through Hezekiah's tunnel (approximately 1/3 mile) which was dug to bring water from outside the city into Jerusalem (2 Kings 20:20).

Cisterns existed throughout Israel, being useful for storing water for the dry seasons. The Law of Moses even provided instructions for their maintenance (Lev. 11:36). Cisterns were carved out of limestone rock and shaped like a bulb with a narrow neck about three feet in diameter then opening to a large bulbous shape. Cisterns were sometimes used as prisons. When Jeremiah was persecuted, he was thrown into a cistern; since it contained no water, he sank in the mud residue that had collected at the bottom (Jer. 38:6–11).

Pools were also used for storing water. Two large pools have been excavated at Gibeon: one is thirty-five feet by fifty-five feet; and the other is round, thirty feet in diameter and sixty feet deep (cf. 2 Sam. 2:13). There was also a pool at Samaria (1 Kings 22:38) and several in Jerusalem (2 Kings 18:17; Isa. 22:11).

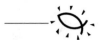

"The Spirit and the bride say, 'Come.' Let each one who hears them say, 'Come.' Let the thirsty ones come—anyone who wants to. Let them come and drink the water of life without charge" (Rev. 22:17, NLT).

# RECREATION AND SPORTS

For ordinary people life involved work; there was little time for leisurely activities, recreation, or sports. Nonetheless, there is evidence that recreational activies existed. Paul drew numerous illustrations from the Olympic games.

## CHILDREN

Archaeology has uncovered children's games in the Mediterranean lands. There is evidence small children had rattles shaped like dolls. Older children played with whistles, balls, marbles, dice, and dolls as well as board games. Small furniture has also been found, suggesting children had dollhouses. In ball games the hand was used for hitting the ball rather than a bat or racquet. Isaiah pictured children throwing a ball as illustrating Judah's captivity in Babylon (Isa. 22:18).

The earliest reference in the Old Testament to games is Genesis 21:9 where Ishmael, a seventeen-year-old is seen maliciously "playing" with or mocking his three-year-old brother, Isaac. The Lord quizzed Job whether he would play with Leviathan (a crocodile) as with a bird, suggesting that children played with birds (Job 41:5). Children also engaged in singing and dancing to the sound of music (Job 21:11–12). Zechariah anticipated the future millennial kingdom when children will once again play peacefully in the streets of Jerusalem (Zech. 8:5).

In New Testament times, children mimicked their parents, playing games of "wedding" and "funeral" (Matt. 11:17).

## SPORTS IN THE OLD TESTAMENT

Jacob is pictured wrestling with the Lord (Gen. 32:24–30). The similar expression ("leg on thigh") depicting the wrestling is expressed in Samson's victory over the Philistines (Judg. 15:8; cf. Gen. 32:25, 33). The men of Abner and Joab engaged in a wrestling contest which quickly became violent (2 Sam. 2:14). Running was common, since there were those who ran before the king's chariot, suggesting they must have trained well (1 Sam. 8:11). Saul and Jonathan are described as "swifter than eagles" (2 Sam. 1:23). Absalom had fifty men running before his chariot (2 Sam. 15:1). Elijah ran some twenty-five miles to Jezreel in outdistancing Ahab (1 Kings 18:46); then, upon hearing of Jezebel's threat, Elijah ran another ninety miles to Beersheba (1 Kings 19:3).

Archery was also practiced (1 Sam. 20:20, 35–38). It is evident that Jonathan had practiced with the bow and arrow. Job felt as though the Lord had used him for target practice (Job 16:12–13).

The sling was used in hunting; David had become very accurate in the use of a sling (1 Sam. 17:40–49). The sling was also a weapon in warfare (2 Kings 3:25). The Benjamites were particularly adept at the sling (Judg. 20:16).

## SPORTS IN THE NEW TESTAMENT

The Apostle Paul drew imagery from Roman sports for spiritual applications. The Isthmian games, held at Corinth every three years, required Greek citizenship for the contestants (cf. 1 Cor. 9:24–27). Paul described the competitiveness of racing in the games. The winner would receive a pine wreath. It was imperative that the runner exercise self-control if he expected to win (1 Cor. 9:25). Paul also mentioned boxing (1 Cor. 9:26). An Olympic boxer who expected to win had to do more than shadowbox. The athlete had to discipline his body to win (1 Cor. 9:27). The verb "I buffet" is taken from boxing and means "I give a black eye to" (1 Cor. 9:27).

Paul emphasized spiritual discipline, illustrated from the athlete's rigorous training. He admonished Timothy, "discipline yourself" (1 Tim. 4:7, NASB). *Discipline* (*gumnaze* ) draws from the athletic scene, picturing the athlete removing his clothing for rigorous training and exercise. At the end of his life, Paul used sports terminology to explain his faithfulness in ministry when he exclaimed, "I have fought the good fight, I have finished the course, I have kept the faith" (2 Tim. 4:7, NASB). In conjunction with this, Paul warned that an athlete must compete according to the rules to win (2 Tim. 2:5).

With the strong emphasis on sports in America, how should Christians view sports? When is it acceptable? When can sports be wrong?

The New Testament illustrates the Christian life as a marathon race (Heb. 12:1–2). The runner is encouraged by those who have previously been successful (Heb. 11), but he must also "lay aside every encumbrance and the sin which so easily entangles . . . and . . . run with endurance the race" (Heb. 12:1, NASB). A race must have a goal; the runner fixes his eyes on the square pillar he is racing toward: "fixing our eyes on Jesus" (Heb. 12:2, NASB). Paul did not want to run in vain (Gal. 2:2; Phil. 2:16). For that reason Paul pressed on, running hard toward the goal for the prize (Phil. 3:14).

Paul used the imagery of the victorious athlete being crowned on the raised platform, the judgment seat (*bema*) to illustrate the faithful believer being rewarded by the Lord (Rom. 14:10; 2 Cor. 5:10).

# BIBLIOGRAPHY

Alexander, Pat. *Eerdmans' Family Encyclopedia of the Bible.* Grand Rapids: Eerdmans, 1978.

Bouquet, A. C. *Everyday Life in New Testament Times.* New York: Charles Scribner's Sons, 1953.

Butler, Trent C., gen. ed., *Holman Bible Dictionary.* Nashville: Holman, 1991.

Edersheim, Alfred. *Sketches of Jewish Social Life.* Grand Rapids: Eerdmans, reprint 1974.

Edersheim, Alfred. *The Temple: Its Ministry and Services.* Grand Rapids: Eerdmans, reprint 1958.

Gilbertson, Merrill T. *The Way It Was in Bible Times.* Minneapolis: Augsburg, 1959.

Gower, Ralph. *The New Manners and Customs of Bible Times.* Chicago: Moody, 1987.

Heaton, E. W. *Everyday Life in Old Testament Times.* New York: Charles Scribner's Sons, 1956.

Metzger, Bruce. *The New Testament: Its Background, Growth, and Content.* New York: Abingdon, 1965.

Miller, Madeleine S and J. Lane. *Harper's Encyclopedia of Bible Life.* San Francisco: Harper & Row, 1978.

Tenney, Merrill C., gen. ed., *The Zondervan Pictorial Encyclopedia of the Bible.* 5 vols. Grand Rapids: Zondervan, 1975.

Unger, Merrill F., *The New Unger's Bible Dictionary*. Chicago: Moody, 1988.

Wight, Fred H. *Manners and Customs of Bible Lands.* Chicago: Moody, 1953.